Historical Associat

The Spanish Civil War

Historical Association Studies

General Editors: Muriel Chamberlain and H.T. Dickinson

China in the Twentieth Century
Paul Bailey

The Agricultural Revolution
John Beckett

Class, Party and the Political System in
Britain 1867–1914
John Belchem

The Ancien Régime
Peter Campbell

Decolonization: The Fall of the
European Empires
M.E. Chamberlain

Gandhi
Anthony Copley

The Counter-Reformation
N.S. Davidson

British Radicalism and the French
Revolution
H.T. Dickinson

From Luddism to the First Reform
Bill: Reform in England 1810–1832
J.R. Dinwiddy

Radicalism in the English Revolution
1640–1660
F.D. Dow

British Politics Since 1945: The Rise
and Fall of Consensus
David Dutton

The Spanish Civil War
Sheelagh M. Ellwood

Revolution and Counter-Revolution in
France 1815–1852
William Fortescue

The New Monarchy: England,
1471–1534
Anthony Goodman

The French Reformation
Mark Greengrass

Politics in the Reign of Charles II
K.H.D. Haley

Occupied France: Collaboration and
Resistance 1940–1944
H.R. Kedward

Secrecy in Britain
Clive Ponting

Women in an Industrializing Society:
England 1750–1880
Jane Rendall

Appeasement
Keith Robbins

Franklin D. Roosevelt
Michael Simpson

Britain's Decline: Problems and
Perspectives
Alan Sked

The Cold War 1945–1965
Joseph Smith

Bismarck
Bruce Waller

The Russian Revolution 1917–1921
Beryl Williams

The Spanish Civil War

Sheelagh M. Ellwood

BLACKWELL
Oxford UK & Cambridge USA

First published 1991

Basil Blackwell Ltd
108 Cowley Road, Oxford, OX4 1JF, UK

Basil Blackwell, Inc.
3 Cambridge Center
Cambridge, Massachusetts 02142, USA

British Library Cataloguing in Publication Data

A CIP catalogue record for this book is available from the British Library.

Library of Congress Cataloging in Publication Data

Ellwood, Sheelagh M., 1949–
    The Spanish Civil War/Sheelagh M. Ellwood.
        p.   cm. — (Historical Association studies)
    Includes bibliographical references and index.
    pbk ISBN 0–631–16617–3
    hbk ISBN 0–631–18048–6
    1. Spain — History — Civil War, 1936–1939. I. Title. II. Series.
DP269.E5 1991
946.081 — dc20

Typeset in 11 on 13 pt Ehrhardt
by Setrite Typesetters Ltd, Hong Kong
Printed in Great Britain by Billings and Sons Ltd, Worcester

For Paul and Gabrielle

Contents

Preface   viii

Principal Dramatis Personae and
Political Organizations   x

Maps   xv

Introduction   1

1   The Antecedents: 1898–1931   5

2   The Second Republic: 1931–1936   13

3   The Rising: 17 July 1936 – 1 August 1936   28

4   A Failed Coup Turns to War: 1 August –
1 October 1936   42

5   The Drive for Madrid: October 1936 – May 1937   56

6   The Republic's Desperate Struggle: May 1937 –
April 1938   75

7   The Third and Final Year: April 1938 – March 1939   89

8   The End of the War. The Aftermath   106

Further Reading   116

Index   121

Preface

The Spanish Civil War is a difficult subject to grasp. The scale and complexity of the issues involved and of the events themselves are such that first encounters with them can be discouragingly confusing. With this in mind, the guiding principles in writing this book have been threefold: to tell the story of what happened in a straightforward way, following the chronological order of events; to present the main players in this complicated drama; and to identify the key social and political issues at stake in the conflict. In this way, it is hoped to help new students of this period of contemporary Spanish history to acquire a clear, basic understanding of the sequence of events; of the people, organizations and institutions involved; and of the interests, beliefs and ideals for which so much blood was shed.

I have deliberately avoided making an extensive examination of certain aspects of the war, such as its international repercussions and ramifications, the role played by women or the development of socialist and anarchist collectives. This is in no way meant to belittle the significance of these (and many other) particular facets of the conflict. On the contrary, their importance was such that the detailed treatment they undoubtedly deserve might well, if given here, muddy the waters of clear summary which I have tried to present in these pages. Readers who wish to flesh out the bare bones of the knowledge they acquire here are referred to the more detailed and specialized volumes suggested in the Further Reading section. The aim of *this* book will have been fulfilled if, on finishing it, readers feel sufficiently confident and interested to want to undertake further study.

I should like to take this opportunity to express my thanks to Professor Muriel Chamberlain, of the Historical Association, and to Ms Alison Dickens, of Basil Blackwell, whose patience and guidance have been much appreciated. I am especially grateful to Professor Paul Preston, of Queen Mary–Westfield College, University of London, and to Dr Helen Graham, of the University of Southampton, for the time they kindly devoted to reading the manuscript in the final stages of its preparation and for the helpful suggestions they made for its improvement. Nevertheless, I take full responsibility for the shortcomings which undoubtedly remain.

The opinions expressed in this book are the author's own and do not necessarily represent those of the Foreign and Commonwealth Office.

Principal Dramatis Personae and Political Organizations

Acción Española: Spanish Action; Alfonsine monarchist cultural and political organization created in March 1931. A journal of the same title was published from December 1931 onwards.

Acción Nacional: National Action; Catholic conservative electoral organization created in April 1931.

Acción Popular: Popular Action; the name adopted by Acción Nacional in 1932.

Alcalá-Zamora y Torres, Niceto: right-wing Republican lawyer and politician. President of the 1930 'Revolutionary Committee'. Prime Minister in the first, provisional, Republican government. President of the Republic between December 1931 and April 1936.

Azaña Diaz, Manuel: left-wing Republican intellectual, political scientist and writer. Minister of War in the provisional Republican cabinet. Prime Minister from October 1931 to November 1933 and from February to May 1936. President of the Republic between May 1936 and February 1939.

Calvo Sotelo, José: leader of Renovación Española. Murdered by Republican police on 13 July 1936.

Casado López, Segismundo: Republican colonel. Led a coup against the Republican Prime Minister, Dr Negrín, in March 1939.

CEDA: Confederación Española de Derechas Autónomas, Spanish Confederation of Autonomous Rightist Parties; coalition of conservative political groups formed in February 1933.

CNT: Confederación Nacional del Trabajo, National Confederation of Labour; anarcho-syndicalist trade union organization.

Companys Jover, LLuis: President of the autonomous regional government of Catalonia.

CT: Comunión Tradicionalista, Traditionalist Communion. Carlist political organization.

FAI: Federación Anarquista Ibérica, Iberian Anarchist Federation; revolutionary wing of the anarcho-syndicalist movement.

FE de las JONS: Falange Española de las Juntas de Ofensiva Nacional Sindicalista, Spanish Phalanx of Committees for National Syndicalist Offensive; fascist coalition formed in March 1934.

FET y de las JONS: Falange Española Tradicionalista y de las Juntas de Ofensiva Nacional Sindicalista, Traditionalist Spanish Phalanx of Committees for National Syndicalist Offensive. Name given to the Francoist single party created in April 1937 by the amalgamation of the CT and FE de las JONS.

Franco Bahamonde, Francisco: Nationalist general with an outstanding military reputation, gained in North Africa. Participated in the rising against the Republic on 18 July 1936. Supreme leader of all the anti-Republican military forces and head of the rebel government and state from October 1936 onwards.

Gil Robles y Quiñones, José María: Catholic conservative lawyer and politician. Leader of Acción Nacional (later Acción Popular) and of the CEDA. Minister of War between May 1935 and December 1936.

Largo Caballero, Francisco: Socialist labour leader and politician. Secretary General of the UGT between 1918 and 1938 and leader of the left wing of the PSOE. Dubbed 'the Spanish Lenin' on account of his radical leftist rhetoric. Minister of Labour, 1931–1933. Prime Minister between September 1936 and May 1937.

Lerroux Garcia, Alejandro: Andalusian politician who made his name as a populist demagogue in Barcelona at the turn of the century. Elected to parliament in 1931 and 1933 for the right-Republican Radical Party. Prime Minister between 1933 and 1935, governing from October 1934 in coalition with the CEDA.

Miaja Menant, José: Republican general charged with the creation of the Committee for the Defence of Madrid in November 1936. Supported the Casado coup in 1939.

Mola Vidal, Emilio: Nationalist general. Director General of Security 1930–1. Leader of the conspiracy which culminated in the 18 July 1936 rising. Killed in an air crash in northern Spain in June 1937.

Negrín López, Juan: Professor of physiology and socialist politician. Minister of Finance between September 1936 and May 1937. Prime Minister from May 1937 to the end of the war.

PCE: Partido Comunista de España, Spanish Communist Party.

PNV: Partido Nacionalista Vasco, Basque Nationalist Party. Largest Basque party; conservative, Catholic and nationalist.

POUM: Partido Obrero de Unificación Marxista, Workers' Party of Marxist Unification. Anti-Stalinist, bolshevist communist party.

Prieto Tuero, Indalecio: Leader of the moderate sector of the PSOE. Minister of Finance in the provisional Republican government of 1931. Minister of Defence between May 1937 and April 1938.

Primo de Rivera y Orbaneja, Miguel: General in the Spanish army. Following a coup in September 1923, presided over a dictatorship which governed in tandem with King Alfonso XIII. Resigned in 1930.

Primo de Rivera y Sáenz de Heredia, José Antonio: Eldest son of the dictator, General Miguel Primo de Rivera. Founder of the fascist party, Falange Española. Executed in a Republican prison on 20 November 1936.

PSOE: Partido Socialista Obrero Espanõl; Spanish Socialist Workers' Party.

Queipo de LLano y Sierra, Gonzalo: Nationalist general. Pro-Republican in 1930–1 but ultimately one of the Republic's fiercest adversaries. Seized Seville on 18 July 1936, thereafter terrorizing the local population through nightly radio broadcasts of singular crudeness and violence.

RE: Renovación Española, Spanish Renewal; conservative monarchist organization created in March 1933. Linked to Acción Española.

Sanjurjo Sacanell, José: Nationalist general. Led an abortive anti-Republican coup in 1932 after which he went into exile in Portugal. Killed in an air crash on his way from there back to Spain in July 1936.

Serrano Suñer, Ramón: Conservative lawyer and politician, married to the sister of General Franco's wife. On arrival in the rebel zone in 1937, he became Franco's closest political adviser.

UGT: Unión General de Trabajadores; General Workers' Union. Closely linked to the Socialist Party.

Varela Iglesias, José Enrique: Nationalist general of Carlist sympathies. Lifted the siege of the Alcazar of Toledo, September 1936, thereafter taking over from Colonel Yagüe the attack on Madrid.

Yagüe Blanco, Juan: Nationalist lieutenant colonel of Falangist sympathies; renowned for the ferocity of the repressive actions carried out under his command (e.g. Asturias, 1934, and Badajoz, 1936). Coordinator of the July 1936 rising in Morocco. Promoted to the rank of general in November 1937.

Maps

1. Republican and Nationalist Positions in October 1936   xvi

2. Republican and Nationalist Positions in February 1939   98

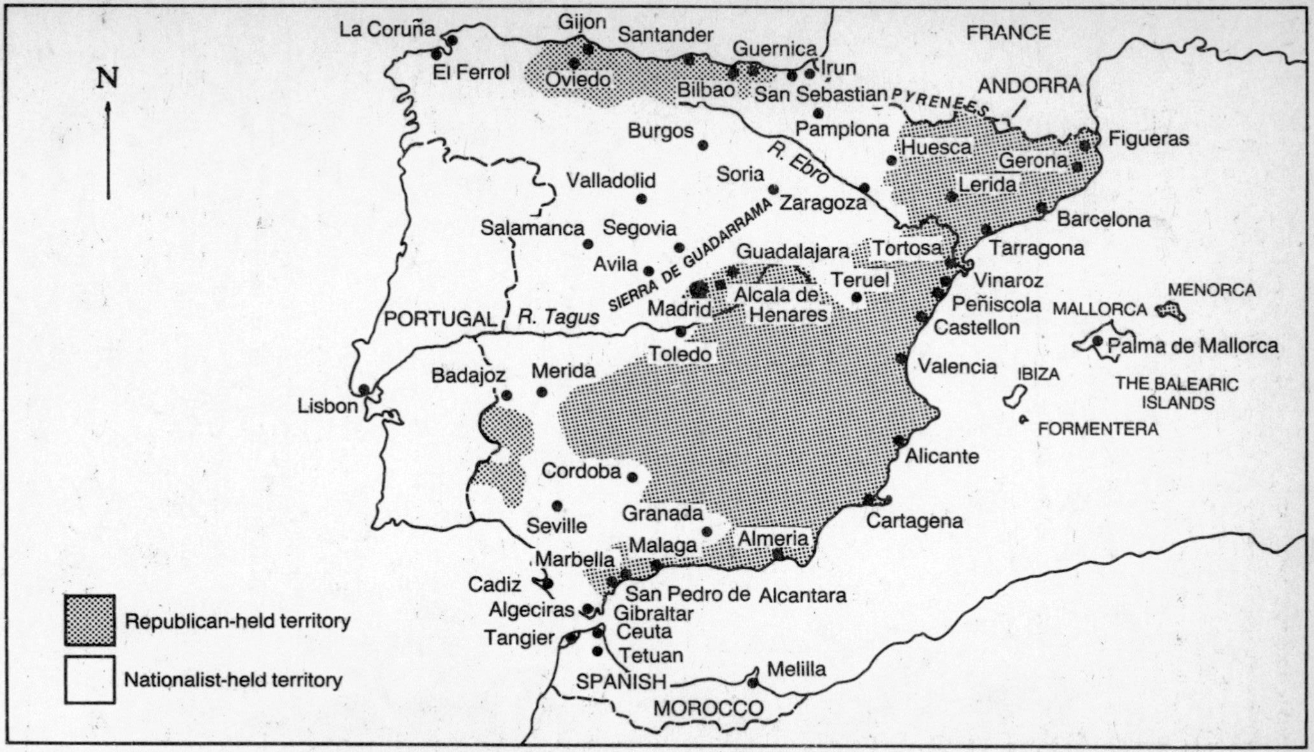

MAP 1 Republican and Nationalist Positions in October 1936

Republican-held territory

Nationalist-held territory

Introduction

All war is horrific, but there is something particularly barbarous about civil war. The twentieth century has witnessed civil conflict in many states world-wide, yet even sensibilities dulled by decades of media, especially television, exposure to violence are still stirred by the events of the Spanish Civil War. The contemporary film footage of frightened, exhausted Spanish refugees crossing the French border in 1939 is still deeply moving; while that of General Franco, signatory of thousands of death sentences, presiding over his Victory Parade in Madrid that same year, is still awesome.

Perhaps it is because there is a certain familiarity about the faces in those pictures that they still strike western observers very forcibly. This was part of modern, industrialized Europe, part of our own social, intellectual, cultural and economic world that was wreaking havoc upon itself. It is not difficult, therefore, to put ourselves in the shoes of those people and to imagine their sentiments. At the time, thousands of outsiders did exactly that. As a result, some were sufficiently concerned to go to Spain and become actively involved in the conflict. Many hundreds died there.

Humanitarian considerations undoubtedly motivated many of those who volunteered to go to Spain, just as they have moved people in subsequent conflicts to varying degrees of solidarity. However, the Spanish war was possibly the first in

1

which ideological solidarity was an integral part of those humanitarian concerns. It was not just that the human suffering in Spain reached the hearts of people elsewhere. The causes of that suffering also touched chords which had to do with particular sets of beliefs and values which were not exclusive to Spain. Thus, in the truculent atmosphere of 1930s Europe, the struggle for hegemony in Spain between the Second Republic and the anti-Republican insurgents was readily translatable into wider European terms as a confrontation between democracy and fascism, or between communism and Christian civilization, depending on one's particular viewpoint. In volunteering to fight in Spain, therefore, foreigners felt that they were not only supporting one or other of the Spanish causes, but also making a stand for a particular set of ideological principles in a universal sense. The enormity of what was at stake for each side was what made the conflict so bloodily intense, for, once initiated, it had to be a fight to the death. Fascism and democracy could not coexist in Spain, any more than they could coexist indefinitely in the rest of Europe.

For all that it is possible to recognize in the Spanish Civil War issues and situations which could also be found elsewhere, it was still essentially a conflict between Spaniards, about Spanish social and political issues, and the product of Spanish history. Francoist propaganda during and after the war harped on the notion that it had been caused by the evil influence of two related 'isms' which were alien (and, therefore, necessarily harmful) to Spain: liberalism and communism. This was, of course, no more true than it would have been for the Republicans to say that fascism caused the war. The purpose of that falsehood was partly to discredit the Franco regime's ideological enemies. It was also to conceal the fact that the war was the result of a conscious decision to overturn the legally constituted democratic order, in the particular interests of some sectors of society, against those of others. There was no foreign involvement in the formulation of that decision. It was not easy, however, for a regime which purported to revere the Fatherland above all else to explain why it had seen fit to subject it to three years of death and destruction. The recourse to external elements was a

2

way of demonizing everything associated with those who defended the Republic. By presenting the latter as the agents of forces alien and hostile to the homeland ('anti-Spain'), the rising and ensuing war became 'justified' as an operation of national 'salvation'.

It is difficult in today's democratic Spain to imagine that, a little over fifty years ago, the country was the scene of terrible bloodshed. Yet the Spanish Civil War remains a cautionary tale, both for Spain and for other countries. For it was, above all, the product of intolerance and fear. At a time when the Middle East is the scene of armed conflict and the transformation of Europe is bringing into the open a varied and vocal collection of hitherto suppressed national, regional, ethnic and religious groups, each with its aspirations, interests and beliefs, the Spanish story serves as a reminder that wars do not simply 'happen'. Conflict can be avoided and peaceful coexistence achieved, if respect for each person's rights and liberties, especially those concerning his or her political or ideological beliefs, is a paramount value. The Spanish Civil War is an example of how terrible the consequences can be when it is not.

1

The Antecedents: 1898–1931

For many years, 18 July was a national holiday in Spain. As the date which marked the beginning of the Spanish Civil War in 1936, it was celebrated by those who had been on the winning side, loathed by those who had not. The war lasted until 1 April 1939. In the intervening two years and nine months, the country tore itself to pieces in a bloody, relentless struggle that left thousands dead, wounded, homeless and persecuted. No one who was living in Spain in 1936 was left untouched by that war, and its shock waves reached far beyond the geographical confines of the Iberian Peninsula.

Although the phrase 'the Spanish Civil War' is generally taken to mean the 1936–9 conflict, this was not, in fact, the first time that there had been civil strife in Spain. From the earliest times, rival tribes, regions, royalists and religions had fought each other for control of the peninsula or, at least, for freedom in their own particular piece of it from domination by others. Indeed, for nearly eight hundred years, from 720 onwards, conflict was the leitmotiv of Spanish history as Christian Spaniards fought to expel the Moslem invaders from North Africa who had begun to colonize the peninsula in 711. This crusade against the Moors — which meant not only the expulsion of people but also the destruction of their culture in Spain — culminated in 1492 with the fall of Granada, the last Moslem stronghold. In that same year, some 150,000 Jews were expelled from Spain after a century of persecution by the representatives of Latin Christianity, which had been declared the state religion of Spain in 589.

By physically liquidating other religions in this way, Spanish Christianity established an unrivalled position in the peninsula. Socially and culturally, this domination was represented and practised by the Catholic Church. Politically, it was championed by the rulers of the Christian kingdoms, in particular by the so-called 'Catholic Monarchs', Ferdinand and Isabella, who by 1492 ruled over the united kingdoms of Castile, Aragón, and Catalonia, as well as the former Moslem caliphates in Andalusia. But it is difficult to sustain social and political dominance unless it rests on a solid economic basis, and by the middle of the fifteenth century, the Spanish state was much impoverished as a result of centuries of conflict. For the Catholic Monarchs, it was therefore a happy coincidence that 1492 also marked the 'discovery' of the New World, the exploitation of whose virtually untapped natural riches helped to fill the coffers of the Spanish treasury for the next three centuries.

The period between 1492 and 1556 saw the creation and expansion of the Spanish overseas empire, largely under the auspices of Ferdinand's grandson and heir, Charles, who was crowned Holy Roman Emperor in 1519 and declared himself 'God's standard-bearer' in the imperial enterprise. Its two principal beneficiaries, the Catholic Church and the Spanish ruling classes, fostered the notion that the 'greatness' enjoyed by Spain nationally and internationally after 1492 was due to the reassertion of Spanish national identity, which was to say *Catholic* identity. Since the Catholic Monarchs were also con-sidered to have forged a united state out of Spain's various kingdoms, it was easy also to equate Catholicism with unity. These four elements — Spanish imperial greatness, national identity, Catholicism and national unity — came to form the basis of conservative ideology in Spain. Any questioning of them from within the country was presented as subversion by those who wished to preserve the status quo, while any change brought about by events outside Spain provoked a state of severe social, political and, one might almost say, psychological

6

crisis in the nation's conservative classes.

It was for this reason that the nineteenth century was especially fraught with internecine tension, as different sectors of Spanish society reacted to two major upheavals: the aftermath of the French Revolution and the collapse of the once-mighty Spanish empire. Both of these were traumatic in themselves, but above all, they signified radical change to the existing order of things in terms of domestic and international affairs. For some, particularly the wealthy land-owning classes who constituted the major part of Spain's political oligarchy and the military elite on whom the former relied to protect their interests, the loss of the overseas colonies and the proclamation of the principles of liberty, fraternity and equality struck at the foundations of Spain's prestige as an international power and spelled a powerful threat to their own privileged existence, based as it was on exploitation, hierarchy and the possession of wealth. For others, by contrast, especially the landless rural day-labourers and the urban working and lower-middle classes who made up the bulk of the population but who had little say in political affairs, these same changes held out the hope of an end to the foreign wars which for decades had depleted their numbers and taxed their pockets and of the introduction of reforms which would distribute wealth and power more equitably.

These two, incompatible, responses to social and economic change also had their translation into political terms. Expressed very simply, the partisans of absolutism, empire, inherited wealth and social inequality gave their support to authoritarian, conservative political groupings, while those who favoured parliamentary rule based on universal suffrage, democratic freedoms and measures to reduce social and economic inequality backed liberal and, from the latter part of the century onwards, socialist formations. In addition, there was a large mass of people, particularly in the rural areas, who subscribed to none of those options but felt a growing antagonism towards a system which excluded, oppressed and exploited them. The nineteenth century was characterized by the strivings for domination of the main political currents, against a background of increasing unrest among the underprivileged rural and urban working classes. On three occasions, the duel between reactionary conservativism and reformist liberalism degenerated into open war,[1] while an endless cycle of (sometimes violent) social protest and brutal repression by the forces of law and order became a constant in Spanish socio-political life.

If the irreconcilable confrontation between those who rejected and those who wanted change was one of the defining characteristics of the nineteenth century in Spain, its other most outstanding feature was the frequency with which military men intervened to alter the normal course of events in favour of one or other of these two camps. Indeed, as one historian of contemporary Spain has observed, such coups — *pronunciamientos*, in Spanish — 'replaced elections as a mechanism for political change'.[2] In effect, their purpose was usually to bring about a change in the nature of the government of the day, but not to install a military regime in place of civilian rule. This was because, on such occasions, the military was not acting to bolster a threatened status quo but, rather, as the instrument of civilian interests too weak or fragmented to impose themselves by their own efforts alone.

One of the principal causes of the rising tide of social and political unrest which successive *pronunciamientos* failed to stem was war-weariness. For centuries, Spain had devoted huge amounts of money and manpower first to gaining and then to retaining its possessions overseas, and to sustaining its monarchs at home. The collapse of the South American empire in 1898, far from heralding a period of withdrawal to winter quarters, provoked quite the opposite reaction, as conservative thinkers, politicians and military men sought ways to 'regenerate' national pride and confidence. In 1906, an international conference assigned the administration of the Sultanate of Morocco to the western powers, with France and Spain playing the dominant roles. The Spanish ruling classes welcomed what they saw as an opportunity to restore Spain's international prestige and to unite a divided country in an overseas enterprise (a method often used by statesmen to divert attention away from domestic dissatisfactions). In the event, Spain's attempts to 'pacify' the portion of Morocco designated as its protectorate were, like all

8

the military campaigns in which it had been engaged previously, a constant drain on the country's human and economic resources, ✳ although it was a source of medals, promotion and prestige for the army officers who served there. The latter constituted an elite body with a strong sense of *esprit de corps*. Isolated from events, families and colleagues in mainland Spain, the officers of the Army of Africa (or *africanistas*) came to see themselves as the heroic defenders of Spanish military honour, charged with restoring Spain's former imperial greatness, which they believed had been lost through the cowardice and incompetence of civilian politicians.

However, the honours and professional advancement which accrued to these officers were largely paid for in the blood, sweat and tears of the conscripts who formed the bulk of the Spanish army and whose social origins were mainly lower-middle and working class, for the sons of the wealthier families could use their money and their connections to buy themselves a commission, a more comfortable posting or even exemption. The human and economic cost of the African war thus aggravated popular discontent with the regime in whose name it was being fought and fuelled the fire of the nascent socialist and anarchist movements.[3] By the 1920s, feelings against the war were running very high among those who bore the brunt of its effects, both at home and abroad. In the summer of 1921, a crushing defeat at Annual, in northern Morocco, cost the Spanish forces over 10,000 men. It was the last straw. In response to massive public outcry and a wave of protest strikes and demonstrations, a parliamentary committee of enquiry was set up to investigate responsibility for the disaster. Rumours began to circulate that the Annual offensive had been undertaken on the personal initiative of the king, Alfonso XIII, without the approval of the Minister of War. Fearing that the publication of such a verdict would tip an already volatile situation over the edge into revolution, the military governor of Barcelona, General Miguel Primo de Rivera y Orbaneja, declared a *pronunciamiento* in Barcelona on 23 September 1923. The king, realizing that Primo had intervened to safeguard the throne, summoned him to Madrid and asked him to form a government.

The monarchy thus remained intact, but power effectively passed to Primo and his cabinet, which was initially composed solely of military men. The parliament (*Cortes*) was closed and political parties banned. The termination of the war in Morocco in 1925 undoubtedly constituted a feather in General Primo de Rivera's cap, but his dictatorship was not popular and the following five years saw a continual increase in the demand for a return to constitutional government. There was, too, growing animosity on the part of liberals, socialists and anarchists, towards a king they considered both inept and frivolous. He was held to be largely responsible for the inefficient running of the Moroccan war and the symbol *par excellence* of a socio-economic system in which the upper classes enjoyed a life of ease and plenty, whilst the working classes barely scraped a livelihood, often working and living in very harsh conditions. Consequently, when in January 1930 General Primo de Rivera asked the country's most important military leaders whether he could still count on them, he discovered that he had alienated the support even of those who had once been his collaborators. King Alfonso – fearing for the stability of the throne – accepted Primo's resignation and subsequent departure to France in self-imposed exile.

The two governments which followed – the first headed by another military man, General Dámaso Berenguer, the second by Admiral Juan Bautista Aznar – still resisted the growing pressure for the restoration of democracy, thereby increasing yet further the unpopularity of the monarchy. Republicanism had been gaining adherents since the turn of the century, and the time now seemed to have arrived when it could offer a viable alternative to the existing regime. Even the king's supporters were aware that the monarchy was treading a knife-edge. When in August 1930, in the northern resort of San Sebastian, a group of Republican intellectuals signed a secret agreement pledging themselves to bring in a Republic, they were joined by a number of liberal and conservative politicians who had previously been partisans of the monarchy but whose

10

disaffection had been growing throughout the 1920s. In October, the Spanish Socialist Party (*Partido Socialista Obrero Español*, PSOE) joined the conspiracy and a 'Revolutionary Committee' was formed. By then, Spain was feeling the effects of the post-war economic crisis which had already shaken the rest of the western world to its foundations. The middle classes feared for their savings and their livelihoods; the aristocrats and bourgeois financiers for their investments. All feared the threat posed by the demands of the militant sectors of the working classes. None had any confidence in the monarchy of Alfonso XIII as the solution to their particular problems.

On 12 April 1931, local government elections were held throughout Spain to test the water, as it were, for a possible return to democratic government at national level. The results indicated that, whilst the monarchy still had control in the rural areas, it had lost it in the cities, which were the nerve-centres of economic, social and political power. Reluctantly, the king left the country as a face-saving way of conceding defeat, and on 14 April 1931, the second Spanish Republic was declared — one of the few occasions in Spain's history until then that change had been effected without military intervention.[4] The members of the 'Revolutionary Committee' formed the new Republic's first, provisional government. In truth, the committee's title was a misnomer, for the leaders of the new regime were, at most, reformist, not revolutionary. Indeed, the moderation of their approach, as perceived by the partisans of rapid and radical socio-economic change, soon became the motive for serious confrontation within the Republican ranks and, ultimately, led to a lack of unity which proved fatal when civil war broke out. In April 1931, however, these divisions had not yet surfaced, and the new regime was greeted with mass rejoicing. The crowds of people who thronged the streets and squares of Spain's largest cities, cheering and dancing as Republican flags were hoisted, were expressing both their delight at the departure of the *ancien régime* and the high hopes for the future that they placed in the nascent Republic.

11

1. From 1833 to 1840, from 1846 to 1849 and from 1872 to 1876, the continuing fight between absolutist principles and liberalism was carried on by the partisans of rival claimants to the Spanish throne. After the death of Ferdinand VII in 1833, the Queen Regent sought liberal support for her daughter, the designated heiress, Isabella. She was opposed by the absolutist supporters of the dead king's brother, Charles, from whom these wars took the name of 'Carlist'.
2. R. Carr, *Modern Spain, 1875–1980*, Oxford, Oxford University Press, 1980, p. 2.
3. The Socialist Party was created in 1879, the UGT in 1882 and the CNT in 1911.
4. The First Spanish Republic was established in 1873, after Queen Isabella had been forced into exile in 1868 and Prince Amadeo of Savoy, having occupied the Spanish throne for three years, abdicated in 1873. It was brought to an end in 1874 when General Pavía declared a *pronunciamiento* which heralded the return of the monarchy in 1875.

2

The Second Republic: 1931–1936

In reality, there was less room for optimism than the scenes of popular jubilation on 14 April 1931 implied. Although none of the king's partisans had raised a finger in his defence when he found himself obliged to go into exile, they had not become Republicans overnight. They were simply bowing before the storm. The essence of their monarchical convictions, however, remained unchanged. They firmly believed that Spain should and could only be governed by a monarch. Many also held that the monarch should rule without a democratically elected parliament, for the values which underlay democratic parliamentarism (essentially the accountability of governors to governed and the right to universal suffrage) were diametrically opposed to their belief in the divine right of kings and the 'natural' hierarchy (i.e. inequality) of the members of a society. The majority of such conservative monarchists were to be found amongst the upper-middle and aristocratic classes who had inherited or accumulated their fortunes under the patronage of the monarchy. Their social status and economic power derived principally from their possession of land, particularly in the south, west and centre of Spain (the huge estates – *latifundios* – of Andalusia, Extremadura and Castile). Their interest in the agricultural exploitation of their land was minimal. They had held sway for decades, aided and abetted by the twin pillars of conservatism in Spain, the Catholic Church and the army.

13

Not surprisingly, these conservative classes were disquieted by a change of regime which did away with the principle of monarchy. The fact that the first President of the Republic, Niceto Alcalá-Zamora, was himself an Andalusian landowner and had twice been a cabinet minister during the monarchy was not enough to allay their fears. Nor was the fact that the 1931 provisional government included only three socialists, Francisco Largo Caballero, Fernando de los Ríos and Indalecio Prieto, the remainder being liberals, bourgeois Republicans and centre-rightists. Even before 14 April, monarchist conservatives were regrouping to face what they assumed would be a hostile new regime. Thus, in the final weeks of King Alfonso's reign, the foundations were laid of an organization whose members saw their mission as the defence of Catholic monarchism: Acción Española (Spanish Action). Ostensibly a cultural organization, Acción Española was, in fact, a hive of political activity which became conspiratorial and anti-Republican when the king departed. More specifically political was Acción Nacional (National Action), formed at the end of April 1931 as a Catholic, conservative, electoral organization. Acción Nacional (which, a year later, changed its name to Acción Popular) was ostensibly a Republican party but initially contained a number of staunch monarchists and was always highly ambiguous in its attitude towards the Republic, claiming that the form of a political regime was merely 'accidental', while what really mattered was its content. In fact, the opposition of the 'accidentalists' to the reform of the status quo severely restricted the Republic's ability to fulfill its own promises and thereby seriously compromised its chances of survival.

Barely a month after the departure of Alfonso XIII came a first taste of the irreconcilable differences of opinion which were to vitiate the Republic throughout its lifetime, making it in a sense the victim of its own commitment to civil liberties, including the right to dissent. On 10 May 1931 a group of Alfonsist monarchists held a meeting in Madrid to create a 'Monarchist Circle'. Apprised of the purpose of the meeting, a crowd of Republican supporters in angry mood gathered outside the building where it was taking place. The failure of the

Minister of the Interior, Maura, immediately to order the police to disperse the crowd angered the monarchists, whilst his decision finally to do so exacerbated the indignation of the Republicans. More fuel was shortly added to the incipient fire. On 11 May 1931, a number of convents and seminaries were ransacked in Madrid, Alicante and Andalusia. Furniture and bedding were thrown out of the windows, and bonfires of religious figures and paintings were made in the streets. These were cathartic gestures through which the arsonists vented the antagonism generated over centuries towards the Catholic Church. For the Church was a socio-economic force which, more than any other, repressed and moulded the average Spaniard's mind and body literally from the cradle to the grave.

The Church's fears that, as an institution, it would come under attack from the Republican reformers were not entirely groundless. The progressive members of Spanish society sought to loosen the iron grip of the clergy on the country's intellectual life, its customs and its morals and, at the same time, to check the Church's enormous economic power. It was not their intention to abolish Catholicism, but it *was* their aim to establish a state network of lay schools, introduce freedom of religious practice for confessions other than Catholicism and make divorce possible. Such ideas were anathema to the Church hierarchy and to many conservative Spanish citizens, to whom the Republic began to appear as little short of an atheistic mayhem. There was also a large number of people who, although not practising Catholics, felt uneasy at the increasingly antagonistic relations between the Church and the Republican government. There was outcry on the right when it was proposed that the new constitution include the separation of Church and state, making the state aconfessional, because this struck at one of the most fundamental beliefs of Spanish conservatism, namely that Catholicism was inseparable from national identity. In the view of the Spanish right, any attempt to change the status of the Church was tantamount to an attack on the nation itself. Thanks to the parliamentary majority of the Socialist and Republican parties, the constitution was approved by the *Cortes* in December 1931, but this result hardened the resolve of those who did not support the Republic more than it strengthened the hand of those who did.

Like the Church, the landed classes were not mistaken in fearing for their possessions. Of all the many inequalities and injustices which the first Republican government had to tackle in order not to disappoint the hopes vested in the new regime, the question of land reform was, at once, the most urgent and the most fraught with difficulties. In addition to the political sensitivity of any proposal to redistribute land in favour of those who had little or none at the expense of those who had more than they needed, there were complex technical considerations to accommodate. It was necessary, for example, to take into account the varying utility of irrigated and unirrigated land; the availability of machinery and fertilizers; the existence of common lands; the kind of agricultural production in different geographical regions; and the relation of family structures and inheritance to the distribution of the land. The thorniest of the problems was the question of indemnity for expropriated landlords. A special commission was set up, in which all the interests concerned — including those of the landowners — were represented. All expropriations were compensated according to the value per hectare declared by the landlords themselves to the property register. This was clearly a fair solution, and it was also a deft political move. For tax reasons, the landowners never registered the true value of their land, but they could not complain that their indemnity was too small without admitting this fraud. Perhaps this strengthened their determination to prevent the Republic's attempt to bring equity to the countryside. From the moment the Law of Agrarian Reform began its passage through the *Cortes* in March 1932, it was effectively blocked by the rightist parties which represented landed interests, such as Acción Nacional and Derecha Regional Valenciana (Regional Right of Valencia).

If the middle-of-the-road liberals who formed the core of the governments of the Republic in its first two years had to contend with serious opposition from the conservative right, they also faced difficulties from the socialist, communist and anarchist left. Even the more moderate of the members and

16

sympathizers of the socialist PSOE and its powerful trade union, the Unión General de Trabajadores (General Workers Union, UGT), the Partido Comunista de España, (Spanish Communist Party, PCE) and the anarcho-syndicalist Confederación Nacional del Trabajo (National Confederation of Labour, CNT) soon felt that the reforming process was proceeding too slowly. After the initial optimism at the birth of the Republic, they began to doubt the capacity of bourgeois liberals to carry through the necessary social and economic transformations successfully. The more radical militants were of the opinion that nothing short of a revolution could enable the working classes to kick over the traces which kept Spain shackled to the Middle Ages in many ways.

The sometimes very bitter internal debate between moderation and radicalism, reform or revolution engaged much of the left's attention and energies throughout the five years that the Republic enjoyed in peacetime. It undoubtedly made a significant contribution both to the objective weakening of the Republic and to the capacity of its adversaries on the right to undermine it even further. An attempted military coup in August 1932 failed to get off the ground, but when general elections were held in November 1933, the parties of the right won, thanks partly to the break-up of unity between socialists and left-Republicans and to the decision of the anarchists to stay away from the polling stations. Once in power, the right immediately set about reversing or disregarding the reforms carried out by their liberal and left-wing predecessors.

Responsibility for the electoral success of the right cannot be laid entirely at the door of left-wing radicalism, however, for a number of other factors also played a part. First, and most importantly, in contrast to the parties of the left and centre, those of the right were united and took advantage of an electoral system which favoured coalitions. In the second place, there was the disillusionment felt by those who had pinned their hopes on the Republic bringing the dawn of a golden age. Their optimism was inevitably dashed on the rocks of reality, in the form of the complexity of the internal problems and the gravity of the contemporary world crisis. Thirdly, Spanish women were given the vote for the first time in November 1933. In large measure thanks to the influence of the Catholic Church on women in Spain, this concession favoured the conservative right more than the progressive left. Finally, the mood in Europe at that time was of a shift to the extreme right, and this had its echo in Spain.

The largest of the rightist organizations was a Catholic co-alition, the Confederación Española de Derechas Autónomas, (Spanish Confederation of Autonomous Rightist Parties, CEDA) formed in February 1933 around Acción Popular. To many contemporaries, it seemed that the CEDA leader, José María Gil Robles, was moulding his party and his policies on fascist lines. Certainly, Gil Robles had many of the traits of European fascism, such as its rabid anti-Marxism, its populism and a vociferous youth movement. However, he was not, strictly speaking, a fascist, for he was also a monarchist (albeit an 'accidentalist' one) and a fervent Catholic, and his message was reactionary, not revolutionary.

Since the creation of the Republic in 1931, there had been a number of attempts to launch groups which *were* overtly and genuinely fascist. They had had little success, however, mainly because the middle classes they sought to attract were too conservative and too Catholic to give their support to an ideology which spoke of socialism and revolution. Nevertheless, in the autumn of 1933, José Antonio Primo de Rivera, eldest son of the late dictator, founded another such party. He conceded that there were similarities between it and the Italian fascist movement, but he was careful to avoid using the word 'fascist' in its propaganda or in its title, Falange Española, (Spanish Phalanx, FE). At the beginning of 1934, the Falange joined forces with an existing extreme rightist organization, the Juntas de Ofensiva Nacional Sindicalista, (Committees for National Syndicalist Offensive, JONS), to become Falange Española de las JONS. It maintained cordial relations with the monarchist intellectuals of Acción Española, and with the latter's political action group, Renovación Española (created in March 1933), but relations with the Catholic conservative CEDA were very strained, for the CEDA occupied the socio-electoral space to which the Falangists themselves aspired.

The period between November 1933 and February 1936, during which Spain was governed by right-wing forces, was dubbed the 'Black Biennium' by the left. The reversal of the reformist trend of the previous two years was exacerbated by the often vindictive reaction of employers and landowners who acted with impunity on their own initiative to reassert their dominant position. Conditions in the rural areas were particularly harsh, and protest was met with armed force. In December 1933, anarchist risings in Catalonia and the neighbouring region of Aragón were put down by force. Later, in June 1934, an agricultural workers' strike was brutally crushed by police and by the Civil Guard, hated by the rural working classes as the repressive instrument of the landlords and the local political bosses (the *caciques*). Even harsher was the reaction to a strike called in October 1934, when the inclusion in the cabinet of three CEDA members (with the highly sensitive portfolios of Labour, Agriculture and Justice) made the Spanish left fear that its organizations were about to undergo the same kind of repression as that suffered recently by their German and Austrian comrades. The government responded by declaring a state of war and calling in the army. This enabled it to put down the strike quickly and to round up the leaders in a number of places, but in the mining area of Asturias in northern Spain, the resistance of the miners turned the strike into a desperate battle against armed police and Civil Guards. Realizing the gravity of the situation, the Minister of War, Diego Hidalgo, called in a man who was not only one of the army's most highly regarded officers but had served in Asturias during the repression of a strike in 1917: General Francisco Franco. From an office in the War Ministry in Madrid, Franco coordinated the deployment in Asturias of a mixed force of regular Spanish soldiers, Spanish Legionnaires and native North African troops. The latter's reputation for brutality was notorious and rightly feared. Asturias was the area from which, twelve centuries earlier, Christian Spaniards had launched the crusade which culminated in the expulsion of the last of the Islamic Arab occupiers from the peninsula in 1492. It was therefore a bitter irony for the

1934 strikers that Moroccan forces should be sent to the only region of Spain never to have succumbed to Arab domination. It was ironic, too, that those forces should be used in what Spanish conservatives saw as a new 'reconquest', with the left playing the part of the infidel this time. The repression of what came to be called the 'October revolution' occasioned hundreds of deaths and arrests among the strikers and dealt a savage, though not mortal, blow to the Spanish labour movement.

The right was quick to present the events of October 1934 as an indication that the country would be taken over by communism if iron discipline were not imposed. For the left, the failure of the strike movement and the repression which followed served to convince them that unity was essential if democracy as they understood it were to survive. It was perhaps in the autumn of 1934 that the first intimation was given of what, two years later, was to be fought out in a civil war. What was at stake was not simply a matter of conflicts between rich and poor, conservatism and progressive thinking, employers and workers, all in their particular and peculiar Spanish context. It was also a question of the wider struggle between democracy and fascism — a process of socio-political polarization whose roots lay in economic depression. In that respect, Spain was part of a confrontation which was brewing throughout Europe. Thus, while the CEDA leader, Gil Robles, regaled his partisans with impassioned speeches demanding all power to be given to him, and the Falange chief, Primo de Rivera, published articles invoking the intervention of the Army to 'save' the Fatherland from the 'pressing anguish' he saw it to be suffering, Chancellor Hitler smashed the socialist movement in Germany, and Chancellor Dollfuss did likewise in Austria. Similarly, just as French socialists and communists had agreed on a plan of anti-fascist action in July 1934, after October Spanish socialists, communists and left-Republicans tried to resist the divisive influence of the most radical elements within their own ranks and to reach an agreement on cooperation in the common interest of the defence of Spanish democracy and a basic programme of socio-economic reforms.

Although the right had secured electoral victory in November

1933, its unity was, in fact, fragile. In October 1935, a financial scandal broke, in which the governing Radical Party was implicated. The Prime Minister, Alejandro Lerroux, resigned and was replaced by a fellow-Radical, Joaquin Chapaprieta. Then, in November, Lerroux was involved in a second scandal which irreparably damaged the image of his party. Rather than assent to Gil Robles' ambition of forming a government, the President of the Republic, Alcalá-Zamora, asked the former Minister of the Interior, Manuel Portela Valladares, to head a caretaker government which would prepare general elections. The *Cortes* was dissolved in the first week of January 1936, and the date for the elections was announced as 16 February.

Convinced that the right could be opposed effectively only by uniting the efforts of left and centre, the reformist sector of the Socialist Party, led by one of the members of the first Republican cabinet, Indalecio Prieto, and the left-Republican parties had been discussing the possibility of working together again since early 1935. In November of that year, with the governing CEDA-Radical coalition entering its death throes, the head of the Republican Left Party, Manuel Azaña Díaz, formally proposed the formation of an electoral alliance with the Socialist Party. The left wing of the party, however, saw this as an opportunity for its rivals in the more moderate sector to gain control of the party. Its contention that the proposed coalition must include the socialist trade union, Unión General de Trabajadores, and youth movement, Juventudes Socialistas, plus the Spanish Communist Party (PCE) and an anti-Stalinist communist party, the Partido Obrero de Unificación Marxista (Workers' Party of Marxist Unification, POUM), was based on the idea that their presence would counterbalance any growth in the influence of socialist moderates. For the PCE, participation in the Socialist-Republican alliance was in line with the policy adopted at the Seventh Congress of the Comintern in August 1935: the formation in each country of 'popular front committees', composed of all the national, anti-fascist forces. Consequently, the alliance formed at the beginning of 1936 by the Spanish socialists, communists and left-Republicans was known as the 'Popular Front'.

Until very late on the day of the general elections, 16 February 1936, it seemed as though the right was going to win again. In the event, although the candidates of conservatism polled more votes than they had won in 1933, the parties of the left still won by a narrow majority. However, because the electoral system was based on proportional representation and because the parties of the right had not formed a grand alliance in the way those of the left had done, the relatively small difference in number of votes became a wide gap when translated into numbers of parliamentary seats. The Popular Front secured an ample majority in the *Cortes*. The leader of the radical wing of the Socialist Party, Largo Caballero, subsequently insisted that the socialists should not participate in the government, because he feared that 'from the heights of the cabinet, the parliamentary wing would have a major moral advantage in the battle for the leadership of the socialist movement'.[1] Consequently, the first Popular Front government in reality consisted only of left and centrist Republicans. The new Prime Minister was Manuel Azaña. The tone of the speech he made on 20 February 1936 and of the new government's programme was of moderation, but this was not sufficient to placate the right, incensed as it was by its defeat.

In the weeks that followed, the rightist press harped incessantly on the idea that the existing social order was in grave danger of disappearing in the wake of a Soviet take-over in Spain. In truth, there were no grounds for believing in the reality of the alleged 'communist threat'. In the spring of 1936, the PCE had no more than 100,000 members, including its youth movement, and only 17 *Cortes* representatives out of a total of 473. Moreover, if the Comintern policy of the 'Popular Front' meant anything, it was co-operation with the moderate middle classes, not revolution. However, the right was not prepared to relinquish power simply because it had lost an election. That defeat had convinced the conservative classes that the political parties which represented them were incapable of ensuring the predominance of their values and their interests within the bounds of the parliamentary system. Consequently, they looked beyond that system for what might be more effective ways of 'saving

22

the Fatherland', as they euphemistically called their desire to hold on to their privileges. They turned to the army and to the extreme, fascist right. Both these options implied the overthrow of parliamentary democracy.

Conspiracies to intervene in the political process by the force of arms had been made and unmade virtually since the declaration of the Republic in 1931. In 1932, for example, General José Sanjurjo had tried to launch a rebellion centred on Seville and Madrid, but it lacked the necessary support within the armed forces and was rapidly quashed. Sanjurjo was imprisoned and ultimately went into exile in Portugal. Undaunted by this failure, a group of monarchists formed a secret 'Conspiracy Committee' to recoup and rechannel anti-Republican feeling. Malcontents in the army created the Unión Militar Española, (Spanish Military Union), with the objective of similar proselytism in the garrisons. At the time of the 'October revolution' in 1934, and again when the *Cortes* was dissolved in 1936, certain generals proposed to effect a coup, with the connivance and active collaboration of right-wing politicians such as Gil Robles, Primo de Rivera and José Calvo Sotelo, leader of the monarchist organization Renovación Española (Spanish Renewal). On the last two of these occasions, what decided the conspirators not to go ahead with their plan was General Franco's contention that the moment was not yet ripe.

This by no means caused the idea of the overthrow of the Republic to be shelved. On the contrary, the conspiratorial meetings which had been going on since 1931 were intensified in the first weeks of 1936. When the results of the February elections were known, military and political leaders on the right attempted to pressure the President and the Prime Minister into annulling them. General Franco, then Chief of the General Staff, claimed that public order was in danger, but the provisional Prime Minister, Portela Valladares, resisted his insistence that martial law be declared, for this would have placed supreme authority in military hands. When Azaña replaced Portela on 19 February 1936, one of his first measures was to post the conspiring generals well away from Madrid and from each other in the ingenuous belief that this would prevent them

23

from engaging in further plotting. Franco was sent to the Canary Islands, Goded to the Balearic Islands and a third suspect, General Emilio Mola, to Navarre in northern Spain, close to the frontier with France.

Even before they reached their new posts, their aides and accomplices had worked out a system of cyphers with which to maintain secret communications. They were thus able to set up a clandestine military committee to coordinate the conspiracy. Headed by General Mola, it had contacts in all the country's main garrisons, with whom it liaised through a secret network of civilian and military messengers. The committee's first plan was to initiate a rising in mid-April, when strategic buildings in Madrid would be occupied, at the same time as garrisons in the provinces would rise. The military plotters had also received assurances from Primo de Rivera that his Falangists would lend their support in the action. In the event, the rising did not take place, because the plot was discovered, but the conspiring continued.

One of the most important conspiratorial centres was the town of Pamplona, the capital of the region of Navarre. This was the heartland of Carlism — the movement which supported the claim to the Spanish throne of the descendants of the nineteenth-century pretender, Charles. It was, therefore, an area of rabid opposition to the Republic. After a considerable amount of negotiation, General Mola secured the support of the contemporary Carlist pretender, Javier de Borbón Parma, and his partisans. Leading Carlists played a crucial role in providing funds for the planned rising, and some were active in the purchase of arms in Europe and their subsequent secret transport to Spain. Indeed, the Carlists had been operating an arms smuggling network across the Pyrenees since 1934. Falangists in the northern provinces also took part in arms trafficking in the first half of 1936. Meanwhile, the national chief of the Falange, Primo de Rivera, imprisoned in March 1936 on charges of illegal possession of arms and insulting the Director General of Security, wrote open letters from his prison cell, in which he urged the 'military men of Spain' to heed the 'call to war which is approaching'.

Although the conspirators undoubtedly felt that the victory of the Popular Front was, in itself, sufficient to justify the rising they were preparing, the instability of the social and political situation in the spring of 1936 added more fuel to their reactionary fire. Street clashes between socialists and Falangists increased in number and violence, sometimes turning into running battles and frequently occasioning deaths or serious injuries. The militant sectors of the working classes were becoming more vociferous and more defiant in response to the economic hardships they continued to suffer, the lock-outs imposed by employers and the apparent inability of the government to resolve the many problems it faced. Both right and left were particularly concerned — though for entirely different reasons — by the strike of building workers organized by the CNT, which lasted several months. The deposition of Alcalá-Zamora as President in April 1936 and the massive, well-organized May Day parades of that year deepened the misgivings of already panicky conservatives.

As spring changed to summer, there was a sudden escalation in partisan violence, which culminated on 13 July 1936 when members of a state police force, the Assault Guards, murdered José Calvo Sotelo. Whilst this was not the origin of the decision to rise against the government, it did act as the immediate catalyst. Angry accusations and open incitations to rebellion were made publicly at Calvo Sotelo's funeral and in the *Cortes* on 14 and 15 July. The leader of the conspiracy, Mola, sent final instructions to his colleagues in those garrisons where rebellion was assured: Manuel Goded in the Balearic Islands, who was immediately to fly to Barcelona and take charge there; Miguel Cabanellas in Zaragoza; Gonzalo Queipo de LLano in Seville; Joaquin Fanjul in Madrid; and Francisco Franco in the Canaries, who was to take command of the forces which patrolled Spain's North African territories. The date of the rising had not been fixed definitively, but all knew it to be imminent. Incomprehensibly, the Republican leaders paid no heed to the information gathered throughout the spring by governmental intelligence services as to the magnitude of what was being prepared, nor to the warnings of their own party members. Azaña, who had replaced Alcalá-Zamora as President of the Republic in May, dismissed the reports as 'scare mongering', whilst the Prime Minister, Santiago Casares Quiroga, over-confidently declared that the government could more than cope with whoever might rise in rebellion.

Whilst the government unwittingly facilitated the preparation of its own demise, the conspiracy entered what were to be its last days of secrecy. To a large extent, the success of the proposed coup would depend on the immediate occupation of Madrid, the seat of state power. The operation was planned as the rapid convergence on the capital of troops from rebel garrisons in the surrounding provinces. The Madrid garrison would also rise. It was by no means certain, however, that this plan would work. In the first place, there were a number of important garrisons, including Madrid, Barcelona and Valencia, where the rebellion did not have the support of the majority of the leading officers. In the second, the elite units of the Spanish army were deployed in Spanish Morocco, and one of the most prestigious generals, Franco, was in the Canary Islands. Since the main body of the navy and the air force were likely to remain loyal to the Republic, the transfer to the mainland of the African forces and the man designated to lead them was as crucial as it was problematic. Thirdly, the government could call upon four armed police forces − the Civil Guard, the Security Corps, the Assault Guards and the Frontier Police (or Carabineers) − to defend the legally constituted order. Whether or not these forces would obey the call was, as yet, an unknown quantity for the conspirators. Finally, there was the pro-Republican civilian population, which could be mobilized by the parties and trade unions of the left, although it was not known at that stage whether the Republican government would agree to distribute arms to the civilian populace.

With these obstacles to contend with, and knowing that the suspect army leaders were under continual surveillance, Mola did not consider, in mid-July 1936, that the optimum moment for the rising had yet arrived. However, an unexpected incident occurred which triggered off a process which quickly became irreversible and ultimately ushered in three years of civil war.

26

Paradoxically, the flash-point of the conflagration was situated where the conspirators had least possibilities of developing the initial impetus and where it might have been expected that the government would have had no difficulty in isolating and suppressing a rebellion: in Spanish Morocco.

NOTES

1. H. Graham, 'Spanish Socialism in Crisis: Politics and Labour 1936–38', in *ACIS Journal*, vol. 3, no. 1, spring 1990, p. 10.

3

The Rising: 17 July 1936 – 1 August 1936

In 1936, Spain had 24,000 of her toughest troops stationed in North Africa. Although the Moroccan war itself had been halted in 1925, Spain continued to maintain a number of garrisons in the area to police the uneasy peace which had been agreed with the native tribesmen. The largest of these enclaves were Tetuán, the capital of Spanish Morocco; Ceuta, on the coast opposite Gibraltar; and Melilla, some 400 km east of Ceuta along the coast towards Algeria.

On 17 July 1936, the officers involved in the anti-Republican conspiracy in the Melilla garrison met to discuss the details of their projected rising in Morocco. Republican police had already carried out searches in some garrisons on the mainland and now, alerted by officers loyal to the Republic, proposed to carry out an inspection in Melilla. The leader of the conspirators there, Lieutenant Colonel Gazapo, tried to prevent the search but, failing to do so and realizing that the plot was about to be uncovered, decided that there was no alternative but to start the rebellion. The commanding officer of the garrison was arrested, as were the chief of the Spanish army in Morocco and all the other officers loyal to them and to the Republic. On the orders of the rebels, Spanish Legionnaires and native Moroccan troops (called *regulares*) occupied the town of Melilla. In Tetuán, the Spanish High Commissioner for Morocco was arrested, martial law was declared, and the town was occupied by rebel troops.

The conspiracy was coordinated in Morocco by Lieutenant Colonel Juan Yagüe Blanco who, in 1934, had been in direct command of the Moorish troops used to put down the Asturian miners' strike. The brutality of that operation had earned him the macabre nickname, 'Hyena of Asturias'. In July 1936, Yagüe had been posted to Ceuta, but distance from the mainland did not prevent him from participating in the anti-Republican conspiracy. When news reached Ceuta of what was happening in Melilla, Yagüe distributed his men strategically throughout the town in preparation for the arrival of government warships, sent to shell Ceuta and Melilla. In the event, they held Ceuta without a fight, for when the naval officers on board the ships attempted to take them over for the rebellion, loyal crew members overpowered the insurgents and sailed the vessels back to the naval base at Cartagena, on the south-east coast of the mainland. Having resisted the government's attempt to nip the rebellion in the bud, the conspirators had taken control in North Africa but had reached an impasse. In the first place, they had very limited means of crossing the Straits of Gibraltar. In the second, General Franco, the man who had been designated to lead the rebel army in Africa, had not yet arrived from the Canary Islands.

Although Franco had been aware of the anti-Republican plot since the early spring, he had been reluctant to commit himself to joining a venture whose success was not guaranteed *a priori*. His opinion carried considerable weight, for his brilliant career at the height of the Moroccan war had won him enormous prestige and respect in military and civilian circles. A strict, Catholic upbringing and long years of military training and service had thoroughly imbued him with the values of his social class: discipline, hierarchy, order and tradition. Yet he did not actively support any political party, for, like many of his comrades-in-arms, he held politicians responsible for what he saw as the decadence of Spain. He was distrustful of the values represented by the Second Republic, such as freedom of speech and association, universal suffrage, political and religious toler- ance and devolution of power to autonomous regional governments. In particular, he believed that liberalism had spawned the ultimate anathema to his own Catholic conservatism – communism – and his handling of the repression of the 1934 revolution in Asturias left no doubt that he considered all means legitimate when the end was the conservation of the status quo. None the less, he had not made any move to save the monarchy in 1931; he had been obedient, albeit without enthusiasm, to the orders of the Republican government; and he had not taken part in either of the two previous conspiracies to overthrow the Republic. Now that the rising was in progress, the rebels waited anxiously to see whether, this time, Franco would join the attempt to overthrow the Popular Front.

In fact, on the day after Calvo Sotelo's murder, Franco had begun to prepare a manifesto to be published at the same time as a state of war was declared. When, in the early hours of 18 July, he received the news of what had happened in Melilla, he immediately sent a telegram to the eight regional headquarters of the army on the mainland and to thirty-one other garrisons. It was undoubtedly intended to confirm his participation in the rising, yet it was phrased in such a way that, had the rebellion failed, it could have been interpreted as being in support of the Republic:

> Glory to the Army of Africa. Spain above all. Receive the enthusiastic greeting of these garrisons which join with you and the rest of our companions on the Peninsula in these historic moments. Blind faith in victory, Long Live Spain with honour. General Franco.[1]

A few hours later, Radio Tenerife broadcast his manifesto, in which he justified the rising as a military duty, in view of the threat to the Fatherland from anarchy, disintegration and absence of authority. Again, there was a certain ambiguity, in so far as he alleged that the Constitution had been 'disregarded and contravened by all',[2] but there can have been little doubt in the minds of those who listened to the radio that morning that Franco was part of a rising against the legally constituted government of the day.

30

At 11 a.m., Franco boarded a small plane which was to take him to Spanish Morocco. It had been hired nearly two weeks earlier in England by the London correspondent of the monarchist daily, *ABC*. He, in turn, was acting on instructions from the paper's owner, Ignacio Luca de Tena, who was evidently confident that Franco would, or could be made to, take part in the rising. After an overnight stop in Casablanca, the plane landed Franco at Tetuán, where he at once took command of the Army of Africa. This gave a great boost to the rebels' morale. In practical terms, however, the major problem of how to transport the Army of Africa across the Straits of Gibraltar remained unsolved.

In mainland Spain, the focal point of the rising was Pamplona, in the northern province of Navarre. There, the head of the conspiracy, General Mola, had few men at his disposal, for most of the regular soldiers were away on summer leave. This lack was soon made up by the hundreds of volunteers who began to converge on Pamplona, in cars, trucks, buses and on foot from all over the province. For Navarre was a Carlist stronghold, and the Carlist militias, the Requeté, had been training in secret camps for months. They now placed themselves under the orders of the rebel military commanders, although they maintained their own distinctive symbols, flag and uniform, with its characteristic red beret. The response of the Carlists to the news of the Pamplona rising on 19 July was so overwhelming that Mola had to ask them to stem the flow of volunteers because the Pamplona garrison had run out of rations to feed them. In Vitoria, too, the capital of the neighbouring province of Alava, the Carlists went *en masse* to enlist at the town's army barracks.

Further south, in the large farming provinces which made up Old Castile, the rising met with few obstacles, and the provincial capitals of Burgos, León, Valladolid, Salamanca, Segovia and Soria were all taken with little difficulty. Castile was the heartland of both Catholic conservatism and fascism, whose paramilitary sections, like the Requeté in Navarre, immediately volunteered for active service against the Republican government. This was not limited to the battlefield. Political

31

and trade-union activists, loyal soldiers and civilian authorities were imprisoned or summarily executed as an immediate follow-up to the military rising. Indeed, in some places, as in the province of Valladolid, opponents were rounded up even before the coup had taken place there. This was a foretaste of the massive repression among the civilian population which was to be part and parcel of military operations when the coup had turned into war. It is significant that it was in Castile, where least fighting took place in the first days and there was never an active front, that the women of the Falange set up an organization whose mission was to provide food and shelter for the civilian casualties of the conflict. The women and children assisted by Auxilio de Invierno (Winter Aid, later called Auxilio Social, Social Aid) in Castile had not been made destitute by military actions but by rearguard repression.

In eastern Spain, a good portion of the three provinces comprising what had once been the kingdom of Aragón was controlled by the troops led by rebel general Miguel Cabanellas. 'His' territory reached from the city of Huesca and the Pyrenees in the north, to the garrison town of Teruel, half-way down the peninsula, and included the important military and communications centre of Zaragoza, half-way between Madrid and Barcelona.

In the north-west corner of the country, in the region called Galicia, as in Castile, the combined efforts of rebel troops and the paramilitary Civil Guard rapidly defeated what opposition could be mustered by the supporters of the Republic. The surrender of the warships anchored at the naval base at El Ferrol (Franco's birthplace) provided the insurgents with an important addition to their arsenal. Eastwards along the coast, however, the northern provinces of Asturias, Santander, Vizcaya and Guipúzcoa were still under government control, thereby assuring the Republic's maritime communications with the outside world. The Basque province of Guipúzcoa was of special strategic importance for it was there, at Irún, that the main road and rail links with south-west France crossed the border. For the time being, the border remained open. Thus, although the northern provinces were separated from the main

32

body of Republican-held territory by a wide sweep of rebel-controlled areas, they were not yet entirely cut off from possible sources of external assistance. For this very reason, the northern front was to be one of the most crucial to the survival or defeat of the Republic.

In the south, General Gonzalo Queipo de LLano and a handful of men had taken Seville on 18 July, while another of the conspirators, General Enrique Varela, had taken control of the port of Cádiz and the coastal area almost as far as Gibraltar. As had happened in Castile, Galicia and Aragón, their task had been facilitated by the active support they received from the Civil Guard, the Falange and the Requeté. The success of the rising in the south had hung in the balance at first, for socialist and anarchist workers' organizations put up a tenacious fight with the few arms they could get together. The Republican government, composed as it was mainly of middle-of-the-road liberals, felt very uncomfortable at the prospect of masses of workers forming organized militias and refused to answer the plea of left-wing leaders to 'arm the people'. It was clear from this that they feared a left-wing revolution more than they feared a military take-over.

While the government dithered, the rebels had managed to begin transporting the Army of Africa across the Straits of Gibraltar by air, and soon the first contingents of Legionnaires and Moroccan native soldiers were landing at Seville and Jeréz. This was important not only on account of the quality of these troops but also because, numerically, their presence on the mainland would tip the military balance decisively in favour of the insurgents. However, with Republican warships patrolling the Straits, and with only six planes available, it seemed impossible to transfer the bulk of these troops to the Spanish mainland. It was vital to the rising that a way be found; and since most of the air force had, as foreseen, remained loyal to the Republic, the only possible solution was to seek foreign assistance. Mussolini at first ignored Franco's requests for aid but finally acceded when approached by Alfonsist monarchists. From Italy, the rebels thus obtained nine Savoia bombers at the end of July. From Hitler, Franco secured twenty Junkers-52 planes.

33

Thus, at the end of July, German and Italian help made it possible to intensify significantly the air ferry between Tetuán and the Spanish mainland. Each plane crossed the Straits several times a day, carrying some two dozen soldiers on each trip. In addition, thanks to the foreign air-cover, the insurgents were able to organize a sea-borne convoy from Africa on 5 August. According to rebel mythology, the Virgin Mary appeared in the Straits and concealed the ships in a mantle of dense fog, thereby giving the first indication that God was on the side of the rebellion. Such 'signs' that they stood for right, morality, justice and, above all, order were to be invoked frequently by the rebels as part of a massive propaganda operation to legitimate the rising as a 'crusade', on the grounds that it had been necessary to 'save' Spain from the 'chaos' into which it had been plunged by the 'godless' supporters of the Republic.

By the end of July 1936, the rising had been successful in the north-west, in the northern half of the central massif and in the south-west corner around Seville and Cádiz. In the rest of the country, either it had failed in the first instance or resistance to it was, as yet, sufficient to maintain Republican control. In Valencia, for example, on the east coast of the peninsula, the rising was to have been organized by General Goded, but at the last minute, it was decided that he should take charge in Barcelona, and General González Carrasco travelled secretly to Valencia in his stead. However, when the moment came to rise, González Carrasco suddenly became hesitant about going through with it. His indecisiveness robbed the coup of the vital elements of speed and suprise, and although the Valencia garrison did eventually rise, the combined efforts of loyal troops and civilians forced it to capitulate on 2 August.

Meanwhile, in Barcelona, the capital of the self-governing region of Catalonia,[3] the rising was in the hands of General Fernández Buriel and other officers of lower rank, pending the arrival of General Goded from his post in the Balearic Islands. When part of the garrison rebelled on 19 July and left its barracks to occupy such strategic buildings as the telephone exchange and the offices of the Catalan government, the troops

34

found that their way to the city centre was barred by Civil Guards and police, under the instructions of the Commissar for Public Order, Federico Escofet. The fact that these two forces did not join the rebellion was a key factor in its failure in Barcelona. At the same time, large contingents of civilians had taken to the streets, particularly in the working-class area around the docks, where one of the largest barracks and the regional headquarters of the army were situated.

Barcelona was then a stronghold of the anarchist movement, whose activists considered that the military rising was the right moment to launch the social revolution they believed would do away with state power and replace it with libertarian communism. Between 19 and 22 July, the CNT and the radical wing of the anarchist movement, the Federación Anarquista Ibérica (Iberian Anarchist Federation, FAI), virtually took over the centre of the city, erecting barricades with sandbags, mattresses and cobbles dug up from the streets, requisitioning buildings and touring the city in cars and trucks painted with the initials 'CNT' and the slogan, 'Uníos hermanos proletarios' ('Unite proletarian brothers'), or its initials, 'UHP'. The Catalan government and a large proportion of the Catalan middle classes had remained loyal to the Republic (not least because they knew that the insurgents, if triumphant, would abolish the Catalan Statute of Autonomy), but the prospect of an anarchist regime which abolished private property and disregarded the established authority of the Republic was totally unacceptable to them. The anarchists aroused further hostility by the revenge some of them took on the Catholic Church, which, for them, epitomized the oppression and manipulation of the poor by the state and its servants. In episodes reminiscent of the church burnings of May 1931, religious buildings were ransacked, effigies piled up and burnt in the streets, and the desiccated corpses of long-dead nuns were put on display outside the churches from which they had been taken.

These scenes repelled law-abiding, middle-class citizens in Catalonia and the rest of Republican Spain, many of whom were Catholic in sentiment and by tradition, even if they were not regular church-goers. They also alarmed the other com-

35

ponents of the loyalist camp. At a time when, in accordance with the Popular Front strategy, moderate socialists and communists were trying to consolidate relations with bourgeois Republicans, the anarchists' revolutionary fervour seemed to confirm the centrist belief that organized working-class power was something to be feared and discouraged. Moreover, the activities of the Catalan anarchists were detrimental to the image held of the Republic by foreign observers, and graphic reports from Barcelona were used repeatedly in rebel propaganda broadcasts as 'proof' that the rising was justified as the only way to 'save' Spain from such rapine. The difference of opinion on the left with regard to what should come first, social revolution or defeating the anti-Republican rebels, was soon to become a source of bitter controversy between anarchists, on the one hand, and socialists and communists on the other. Indeed, it led to a war-within-the-war which seriously weakened the Republican cause and contributed in no small measure to its ultimate defeat.

By 20 July, the military rising in Barcelona had been put down and its leader, General Goded, arrested as soon as he arrived from Palma de Mallorca. The anarchists, however, did not consider their revolution over. They dominated the Committee of Anti-Fascist Militias set up in Barcelona on 21 July and, by virtue of their control of the streets, seemed set to become the real masters of the city, beyond the authority of the Catalan government. Three days later, amid scenes of tremendous euphoria, the first of a number of volunteer columns left Barcelona for Aragón by rail and in a motley collection of cars, buses and trucks. Armed with their enthusiasm and the weapons they had seized from the army barracks they had stormed, the Durruti column (so named after its anarchist leader, Buenaventura Durruti) set off in a long, straggling caravan. It was bound for the capital of Aragón, Zaragoza, another centre of anarchist strength which, unlike Barcelona, had succumbed to the superior strength of the rebel troops. By the end of July, some 20,000 men had left Catalonia for Aragón.

While Barcelona saw the military rebellion succeeded by a struggle for control between the anarchists and the Catalan government, the state capital, Madrid, was the scene of confusion of a different sort. There, the conspiracy had numerous adherents, but no clear, single leader. The situation created when news of the rising in Morocco reached the city's barracks was one of tense expectation. In theory, the plan was for the city centre to be taken by General Fanjul from the Montaña barracks, close to the presidential palace, and for General García de la Herán to control the outskirts from another barracks situated in the working-class district of Carabanchel, on the south-west flank of the city. They, in turn, would receive air-support from the nearby Getafe and Cuatro Vientos airfields. In practice, things went differently. García de la Herán's rising in Carabanchel was aborted, and he was immediately shot. The majority of the pilots at Getafe and Cuatro Vientos remained loyal, and at the Montaña barracks, Fanjul was besieged by some 2,500 Civil and Assault Guards, two battalions of leftist volunteers, a section of loyal artillery troops and a field gun. In addition, there were hundreds of civilians, armed with some of the 5,000 rifles which, against the instructions of the government, had been handed out by a group of artillery officers on the afternoon of 18 July. When the defenders of the Montaña barracks surrendered, the Civil Guards who were to occupy the building were unable to prevent the armed masses from rushing in. General Fanjul was arrested by Assault Guards, but hundreds of other officers and men died at the hands of incensed civilians. As in Barcelona, this incident was widely publicized by the rebels as an illustration of leftist bestiality and frightened the moderate sectors of the Republic's own support.

About one kilometre away from where the Montaña barracks was under siege, the President of the Republic, Manuel Azaña Díaz, received news of developments in what had once been the Royal Palace. 'He was very composed and serene', said a supporter who talked with him on the morning of 20 July.[4] However, the President and his collaborators showed no sign of relief or optimism when they knew that Republican forces had gained the upper hand in Madrid. In the first place, they knew that the rising had triumphed in large areas of the rest of the country. In the second, a profound political crisis had been opened by the rebellion, which revealed the underlying weakness of the Popular Front coalition and presented a serious challenge to the stability of the bourgeois Republican regime. On 18 July, Azaña had proposed the formation of an all-party cabinet, but this had met with the opposition of the anarchist CNT, the socialist trade union (UGT), the socialist youth movement and the leader of the left wing of the Socialist Party, Francisco Largo Caballero.

On 19 July 1936, unable to contain the rising or to provide a solution to the internal political impasse and unwilling to arm the civilian populace, the Prime Minister, Santiago Casares Quiroga, resigned. He was succeeded by Diego Martínez Barrio, who tried unsuccessfully to reach agreement with the director of the conspiracy, General Mola. The conditions he offered were the constitution of a cabinet which would include military men and conservative politicians, in return for an end to hostilities. Mola is said to have replied, 'You must be loyal to your people, as I shall be loyal to mine' and, shortly afterwards, declared martial law in Navarre. Even though Martínez Barrio's attempt failed, the news that it had been made at all prompted fresh criticism from the left, whose militants demonstrated in protest in Madrid. After only a few hours in power, Martínez Barrio also resigned, to be replaced by a close personal friend of Azaña, José Giral, who until then had been Minister of the Navy.

The failure of the rising in the capital was a major setback for the rebels, but it did not mean that the forces defending the Republic could rest on their laurels. On the contrary, while it had been relatively easy to overcome the attack launched from within the city, it was now necessary to prepare adequate defences against a much more redoubtable attack approaching from those provinces to north and south where the rising had been successful. The immediate threat came from the north. In Navarre, a column of Carlist volunteers had left Pamplona on 19 July, with the aim of reaching Madrid by 25 July. This date was chosen because of its religious and patriotic significance, for it was the feast day of St James, patron of Spain and symbol of the Christian reconquest of the country from Moslem domination. For the Carlists, the rising against the Republic was a new war against the heathen. Similar columns, made up of rebel soldiers and Falangist volunteers, had also left Burgos and Valladolid in Castile. On 21 July, the Castilian and Navarrese columns joined forces at Soria, high on the Castilian plateau, 230 km north-east of Madrid. Together, they continued their march towards the capital, with the intention of relieving the garrison at Guadalajara on the way. There, not 50 km from Madrid, the rebel commander, Joaquin Ortiz de Zárate, was under heavy attack from loyal Republican troops and volunteer militiamen.

In a desperate attempt to nip the rising in the bud, the government had issued a series of decrees dismissing rebel officers from their posts and releasing rank-and-file soldiers under their command from their oath of obedience. All that this achieved was a tremendous state of confusion among loyal units, while those which had rebelled simply ignored the government's measures. In the light of what amounted to the dissolution of the armed forces, the parties and trade unions of the left immediately set up recruiting posts, where their respective members enlisted and were organized into impromptu divisions and battalions. Many of the volunteers had no military training beyond what they had received during their term of military service. Uniforms were scarce, as were arms and munitions. Uneven lines of men doing 'square-bashing' in civilian clothes or, at best, in boiler suits (the 'uniform' of the Spanish working man) became a familiar sight in the parks, schoolyards and barrack forecourts of Republican-held cities. What they lacked in military style they made up for with courage, conviction and enthusiasm.

The government was less than comfortable with this sudden upsurge of a 'parallel' army, but with the regular army in disarray, it had no alternative but to tolerate the militias. Once the rising in Madrid had been brought under control, however, the government began to reorganize its army, with the creation of new battalions. The immediate objective of the War Ministry and the General Staff was to coordinate the regular army and the party militias in a concerted attempt to detain the advance

39

of the enemy columns from the north. Both the Republicans and the rebels were intent upon reaching the passes through the mountains which ran from north-east to south-west some 50 km north of Madrid, for whoever occupied these routes would then be in control of immediate access to the capital from Galicia, Vizcaya and Castile. On 21 July 1936, a column of men left Madrid for Alcalá de Henares and Guadalajara. In both towns, they suppressed the rising, and in Guadalajara, the leading officer, Ortiz de Zárate, was shot. Here, as had happened in Barcelona and Madrid, the fact that the Civil Guard did not support the rebellion was decisive to its failure. News of this reverse for the insurgents temporarily halted the advance of Colonel García Escámez's column from Pamplona. A second Republican column headed for the pass which took the main road to the north-west into the Castilian plain, while a third occupied the secondary road to Segovia at the Navacerrada pass. A fourth, reinforced with Civil Guards, set out for Avila, and a fifth received orders on 22 July to proceed to the Somosierra pass, almost 100 km to the north-west of Madrid, on the main road to rebel-held Burgos.

Throughout the dry, sweltering month of July, the Sierra de Guadarrama was the scene of intense fighting, with many casualties on both sides. The Republican government continually sent what reinforcements it could to this crucial front, but they were always insufficient to encircle the enemy's relatively unguarded flanks. The Republican militias resisted valiantly, but they had neither the experience nor the discipline of their adversaries. Whereas the left-wing volunteers had received little or no training prior to 18 July 1936 and had few arms at their disposal, the rightist militias had been receiving military instruction for months. The Carlists and Falangists drilled at secret camps in Spain, while the Alfonsist monarchists had, on occasion, sent men to Italy for training. Moreover, while the right-wing volunteers unquestioningly obeyed military orders, the Republican militiamen owed their first allegiance to their respective party or union leaders and gave second place to military discipline. This frequently led to conflicting opinions when an operation was proposed. Anarchists are said to have left their positions on more than one occasion to take a vote on whether or not to attack.

On 27 July, the rebels took control of the most northerly of the passes, at Somosierra, forcing the Republicans to retreat. With the occupation, on 1 August, of the village of Guadarrama, at the foot of the pass at the southern end of the mountains, it looked as though it would only be a matter of days before the rebels reached Madrid. Yet the Republican defences held up sufficiently to keep the capital beyond the enemy's grasp. Indeed, it was for precisely that reason that what had begun as a military coup now turned into a war; and a war in which no one could claim neutrality. While many people found themselves on one side or the other simply by dint of where they happened to be on the day of the rising, many more consciously and actively supported one or other of the opposing armies for ideological reasons. In the same way that, for the first time ever, the Republic had given the mass of the Spanish people access to and a voice in their country's political life, the conflict which now threatened to end that regime also involved everyone.

NOTES

1. Quoted in L. Suárez Fernández, *Francisco Franco y su tiempo*, vol. II, Madrid, Fundación Nacional Francisco Franco, 1984, p. 52.
2. Ibid., p. 53.
3. Catalonia had been granted a Statute of Autonomy in 1932. It was temporarily suspended in October 1934, after the President of the Catalan Government (the *Generalitat*) had declared Catalonia an independent state within the Federal Republic of Spain, but was soon restored. The anti-Republican right was radically opposed to any devolution of central power, on the grounds that this was tantamount to 'dismembering' the Spanish state.
4. Eligio de Mateo, interview with S. Ellwood, in D. Solar (ed.), *La guerra civil española*, vol. 4, Madrid, Historia 16, 1986–8.

4

A Failed Coup Turns to War: 1 August — 1 October 1936

By the end of July 1936 what had been planned as the rapid seizure of the nerve centres of power had become a war between two armies and two civilian populations. It was also turning into a war between two states within one country. In the rebel zones a military regime was instituted at once, whereas in the Republican-held areas the civilian character of the legally constituted regime was maintained until the end of the war. The general imposition of martial law declared by the insurgents on 28 July 1936 was gradually extended as their forces advanced, not to be lifted until 1948 — nine years after hostilities had ended. The Republican authorities, by contrast, strove to maintain the structures and functions of democratic rule and did not impose martial law in their zone until the conflict was in its final stages.

While the legitimate government expended time, energy and authority on cabinet crises and internal tussles with anarchists, communists and radical socialists, the insurgents quickly established a committee of military leaders to control and coordinate front-line and rearguard action. Headed by General Cabanellas, the Committee for National Defence was composed entirely of military men. Although they needed and accepted the active support of the political parties of the right and most of them held political opinions in sympathy with those parties, they were disdainful and distrustful of party politics and career politicians. Considering the coup and, even more, the ensuing war as an essentially military affair, they excluded civilians from the decision-making processes of its conduct. On 24 July, the Committee issued its first manifesto, in which it explained the motives for the rising. That same day, General Franco, still in Spanish Morocco, was appointed chief of the Armies of Morocco and Southern Spain. He was shortly able to make his appointment effective. On 6 August, he landed in Seville, where he established his general headquarters.

The stage was now set for the initiation of the northwards march on Madrid. On 2 and 3 August, two columns of Legionnaires and native Moroccan troops left Seville. They headed north-west, towards Extremadura, a desperately poor and backward region of Spain whose mainly agricultural population had long suffered the social and economic hardships occasioned by climatic extremes, absentee landlords, unemployment and the grossly unjust distribution of land. The rebels' immediate objective was the town of Mérida, an ancient Roman settlement in the province of Badajoz and an important crossroads between north and south, Madrid and the west. Here, they hoped to link up with General Mola's troops advancing south through Old Castile. This was a crucial manoeuvre for, if it were accomplished, the northern and southern areas of rebel territory would be united, and a concerted effort could then be made to take Madrid from the west, along the valley of the River Tagus.

The two columns advanced very rapidly. The training and discipline of the African troops were more than a match for the badly coordinated and ill-armed columns of Republican militiamen who were their adversaries. The psychological effect of using Moroccan troops also played a significant part. Their horrific reputation for savagery went before them. Indeed, many of the militiamen of 1936 had already seen in October 1934 that it was not exaggerated. By 10 August, they had reached Mérida, which surrendered that day after heavy fighting. They were then joined by a third column, and the three were amalgamated as the 'Madrid Column', under the command of the veteran of Africa and Asturias, Juan Yagüe. Yagüe's for-

43

midable column now marched west to complete the rebel control of Extremadura with the occupation of the provincial capital of Badajoz.

The assault on the town began on 13 August 1936. The defenders — some 500 regular soldiers and 3,000 militiamen — put up a desperate fight and even attempted a counter-attacking operation, which failed for lack of men, officers, supporting operations and arms. The rebels responded with bayonet charges and hand-to-hand combat. Carried on at the height of the summer in one of Spain's hottest, driest regions, the fighting was extremely bloody, but the repression which followed the fall of Badajoz on 14 August surpassed anything that happened on the battlefield. Surviving members of what, by then, were being referred to as the 'Nationalist' forces still deny that there was any carnage at Badajoz, alleging that such a thing would not have been Christian. The evidence given by foreign newspaper correspondents and by people who lived in the town at the time overwhelmingly contradicts this version. It is no exaggeration to speak of the 'Badajoz massacre'. According to one eye-witness, the bodies of hundreds of Republicans killed in the fighting were burned in the cemetery. Hundreds more people were herded into the bullring and shot. It was, indeed, ironic that the war of which this slaughter was part had been initiated, allegedly, to save Spain from the 'barbarity' of the 'atheistic hordes' which were supposedly about to invade Spain from eastern Europe.

The fall of Badajoz and, with it, the conclusion of the campaign in western Andalusia and Extremadura stimulated the offensive spirit of the Nationalist forces and consolidated the prestige of the man who had directed the operation, Francisco Franco. Convinced that they were an invincible army and that ultimate victory was at hand, the column under Lieutenant Colonel Yagüe's direct command was now poised to begin the advance on Madrid.

While the main theatres of war in the first weeks were the Sierra de Guadarrama and Extremadura, secondary fronts were being established all over the country, as the Republican government recovered from its initial confusion and began to organize the troops and militias at its disposal to resist the impetus of the Nationalist advance. In Aragón, there was continual fighting around the three main towns of Huesca, Zaragoza and Teruel. In Asturias, the insurgents were besieged in their barracks in Oviedo and Gijón, while the Republican forces in turn were under fire from Nationalist warships off the coast of Gijón and, inland, from troops positioned to the south of Oviedo. In the south, General Queipo de LLano turned his attention to eastern Andalusia, to advance on Córdoba, which still held out against the rebels.

Off the east coast, the rising in the Balearic Islands had been successful on Ibiza, Formentera and Mallorca, but not on the island of Menorca. On 7 August 1936, a two-pronged expedition left the ports of Valencia and Barcelona with the aim of recovering the first three islands. The attempt was only partially successful. By 16 August, Ibiza and Formentera had been reoccupied by the Republicans, but they had managed to secure only a foothold on the north-east coast on the main island of Mallorca. All three islands were soon under Nationalist control again; Menorca held out until February 1939. Finally, on the coast of the Bay of Biscay, San Sebastian came under threat in the first week of August as rebel forces from Navarre pushed northwards to take the area adjacent to the French border. If successful, they would achieve two important goals: to reduce by half overland communications between Republican Spain and democratic Europe and to isolate the industrial and mining areas of the north from the rest of the area controlled by the government. Without the coal and steel of Vizcaya and Asturias and with only the Catalan route open to receive munitions and other supplies from outside, the Republic's capacity to provide its armies with such vital commodities as arms, munitions, fuel and spare parts would be severely handicapped.

Both objectives were important. By the end of July, the Nationalists held the principal agricultural areas of the south-west, north-west and north-central regions, while the Republicans had retained the principal industrial and manufacturing areas of Madrid, Vizcaya and Catalonia, plus the agricultural areas of eastern Andalusia, Murcia, Alicante and Valencia.

With regard to communications, the rebels had taken the ports of Galicia and held the territory next to the border with Portugal, but the Mediterranean and Cantabrian coasts and the all-important road and rail links at either end of the Pyrenees were still in Republican hands. Thus, the two sides were fairly evenly balanced, and the Republicans perhaps even had a slight advantage. Consequently, the situation was particularly sensitive to any development which might alter this unsteady equilibrium.

In aiming for the border area of San Sebastian, the Nationalists drove at the Achilles' heel of the Republican war effort. International reaction to the rising showed early that it was from outside Spain that the Nationalists could expect to derive major advantages. In the first place, their natural ideological allies, Nazi Germany and Fascist Italy, were willing from the outset to provide active support in the form of technical expertise, troops, arms, vehicles and munitions on favourable credit terms. In the second, the western democracies were reluctant to become involved in the Spanish conflict. Although France (where a Popular Front government had been established in May 1936) was at first willing to supply the Republic with aircraft, it reversed this policy within a few weeks, on account of the disquiet it provoked in British government circles. The political situation in Europe was weighted against the Republic, for the main concern of the west European democracies was the increasing power and belligerence of the German Chancellor, Adolf Hitler. This was also a factor in the foreign policy of the Soviet Union. The Spanish ambassador in Moscow, Marcelino Pascua, reported his impression that Russia's desire to maintain good relations with Britain would always take precedence over any feeling of anti-fascist solidarity with the Spanish Republic. Anxious to avoid a war with Germany, the British government warned the French Prime Minister, Léon Blum, that, should France enter the Spanish war in support of the Republic, Britain could not guarantee to assist France in the event that German aggression were to be directed against France as a result.

It was a compelling argument, which Blum was forced to

accept. The democratic powers could not, however, publicly wash their hands of the Spanish war without losing a considerable amount of face and credibility. On 1 August 1936, France put forward a compromise solution to the dilemma; the adoption of a policy of non-intervention in Spain, on the grounds that the conflict was a purely internal matter. Four days later, the US government expressed its agreement with the policy of non-intervention, and by 7 August, the French proposal had been signed by Britain, Belgium, Holland, Poland, Czechoslovakia and the Soviet Union. By 15 August, France and Britain had prohibited the sale of arms to Spain; the USSR following suit two weeks later. Germany, Italy and Portugal stated their agreement 'in principle' with non-intervention, and Germany signed the pact on 24 August.

In practice, even as the non-intervention negotiations were going on, both Germany and the USSR were preparing to establish their respective bridgeheads in Spain. Fearing that the Republic would rapidly collapse under the combined weight of international isolation and anti-Republican aggression, Stalin decided on active intervention in the conflict. On 25 August, Vladimir Antonov Ovsenko arrived in Barcelona to take up his appointment as Soviet Consul. Two days later, the new Russian ambassador, Marcel Rosenberg, arrived in Madrid, accompanied by a sizeable team of aides and advisers. At almost exactly the same time, Hitler had decided to increase his aid to the Nationalists, although, for the time being, it was to be limited to arms and the personnel strictly necessary to train Spanish forces to use them. German troops were not to take part in the fighting except in the event of extreme necessity and then only with Hitler's express permission. The caution surrounding the increase in the provision of material aid was largely a function of Germany's own rearmament programme; none the less, Hitler's assessment was that it might be necessary to increase further German involvement in the Spanish war and that, therefore, closer on-the-spot surveillance was required. Accordingly, towards the end of August 1936, the chief of the German secret intelligence service, Admiral Canaris, made the first of many trips to Spain, and Lieutenant General Walter

Warlimont arrived in the peninsula to 'act as the representative of the German armed forces before Franco . . . serve as adviser to General Franco with regard to his possible future requests for further aid . . . and bear in mind that military support for Spain should be compensated by the supply of Spanish raw materials'.[1]

In their unwillingness to become embroiled in the Spanish war, the western democracies were undoubtedly influenced not only by the international situation but also by the confusion and instability they perceived in the Republican camp. We have already noted the three changes of Prime Minister which occurred in the space of as many days in mid-July and the increasing degree to which successive Republican cabinets were overwhelmed by the pressures exerted on them from the left by socialists, communists and anarchists — forces which, moreover, were split amongst themselves into various antagonistic factions. Indicative of the enormous strain under which cabinet members worked were the signs of exhaustion which began to show in the Minister of War, General Castelló, towards the end of July. He was replaced by Colonel Saravia on 5 August 1936, but this was no more than a pragmatic solution to an immediate problem. The real crisis lay in the fact that the centre-Republican government had lost control of the political situation. Most contemporary observers, of all ideological positions, are agreed that real power was in the streets, not in the ministerial offices nor, even less, in the presidential palace. On 4 September 1936, the government headed by José Giral fell. The new Prime Minister was the leader of the left wing of the socialist party, Francisco Largo Caballero. His cabinet included left-Republicans, socialists and communists in an attempt to provide a government which was a true reflection both of the forces composing the Popular Front which had won the last elections and of the real contemporary balance of power. While this was a necessary first step towards returning political control to the executive body, it did little to dispel the misgivings of conservative governments outside Spain. They made little distinction between anarchists, anti-Stalinists, pro-Stalinists, radical socialists, moderate socialists and left-Republicans. To them, all were 'reds', and although they perceived the threat which Hitler and Mussolini posed to parliamentary democracy, they were not prepared to risk aiding communism in order to defeat fascism.

Both nationally and internationally, the democratic credibility of the Giral government had been seriously eroded by the murder, on 23 August, of a number of people who were being held in Madrid's Model Prison as known or suspected right-wingers. These executions, provoked by the Badajoz massacre, were the more horrific for the apparent inability of the government to prevent them. Even more damaging to Giral was the military progress of the war. Throughout August, the Nationalists pressed towards Irún, between San Sebastian and the French border, while the Army of Africa drew ever closer to Madrid from Extremadura. The Republican militias fell back in constant retreat as Yagüe's Legionnaires and Moroccan *regulares* drove relentlessly forward. When, on 3 September 1936, news came that the Nationalists had reached and taken Talavera de la Reina, 114 km west of Madrid, it seemed that the fall of the capital must be imminent. Although this was the catalyst for the resignation of the Giral cabinet, it also marked the point at which a brake was put on the Nationalist advance. With Madrid as the only place left to retreat to, the Republican troops and militiamen had their backs to the wall. The leader of the First Division of the Republican army, General Riquelme, had predicted despairingly that this forces would 'only stop running when they have nowhere left to run to', and this was exactly what happened. The Nationalists continued to advance, but far more slowly and at greater cost in men and munitions from the beginning of September onwards.

As it became clear that Madrid would not, after all, capitulate in a matter of days, Nationalist attention focused on the city of Toledo, some 70 km, south-west of Madrid. Once the hub of the Spanish empire, Toledo was still the religious capital of Spain, and its enormous fortress, the *alcazar*, housed the military academy for infantry cadets. The city had enormous ideological and emotional significance for the partisans of the Nationalist cause. It was the symbol of all they held most dear and all they believed to be under threat from the Republic: Catholicism, the greatness of Spain as an international power, military strength as the supreme arbiter of political destiny. On 21 July, the military governor of Toledo, Colonel José Moscardó, had risen against the Republic. However, the resistance of loyal troops and townspeople forced him and about 1,000 soldiers, Civil Guards and Falangists to take refuge in the *alcazar*. With them went some 600 women and children and 100 people of known left-wing sympathies, taken hostage by the rebels. Throughout July and August, Republican forces laid siege to the fortress, but despite continual and intense artillery bombardment and dynamiting of its foundations, it did not collapse. Its beleaguered occupants suffered heavy losses and, by the beginning of September, were virtually without food, water or medicaments. None the less, they refused to surrender, believing that Madrid would soon fall and the war would then be at an end.

In Talavera de la Reina, 90 km to the west of Toledo, Yagüe was anxious to press on to Madrid. General Franco, however, held a different view and, on 21 September 1936, ordered him to make a detour to Toledo to relieve the besieged *alcazar*. Yagüe disagreed with this decision. He was immediately relieved of his command, and General Enrique Varela took over. On 27 September, the Army of Africa occupied Toledo, and the siege of the *alcazar* was lifted. The emaciated survivors embraced families and friends in highly emotive scenes in the rubble-strewn streets. General Franco himself visited the city two days later and was given an ecstatic reception as the saviour of the 'martyrs' of the *alcazar*.

This episode revealed a number of things about General Franco's character which were to be visible many times in later years, during his forty-year dictatorship. First, he would not tolerate any questioning of his decision. Yagüe was an experienced soldier and, like Franco, had served in Africa. For both those reasons, Franco respected him. Yagüe, however, was under Franco's command. The advance on Toledo was not a matter for discussion between equals; it was an order, given by the superior, to be obeyed by the inferior. For Franco, hierarchy and discipline were paramount. Secondly, the relief of the *alcazar* showed that Franco appreciated the value of public relations exercises for enhancing his own stock. He was not an especially religious man, nor was he noted for his humanitarian concerns; and Toledo was irrelevant to the military progress of the war. Franco knew, however, that if he were responsible for the deliverance of so important a symbol of the religious and historic essence of Nationalist Spain, he would stand head and shoulders above the rest of the rebels, whose only concern was to take Madrid. As we shall see, his assessment was both accurate and apposite. Thirdly, the way he organized the achievement of this goal demonstrated his cautious cunning. He did not lead the rescuing troops himself, thereby running the risk of being wounded or killed. He gave the orders, then made a triumphal entry when the dangerous part was over. Probably no one realized it in September 1936, but Toledo provided a glimpse of Franco the statesman as well as Franco the soldier: authoritarian, calculating and deeply self-centered.

Not surprisingly, the siege of the *alcazar* of Toledo came to constitute one of the principal myths of the Nationalist history of the civil war, representing the supposed martyrdom of Christian values at the hands of international atheism. The Catholic Church seized upon Toledo as the symbol of the struggle between Good and Evil it believed the whole war to be. On 28 September, the day after the siege was lifted, the Bishop of Salamanca, Pla i Deniel, expressed this Manichean view of the war and what lay behind it in a pastoral letter entitled 'The Two Cities', after the Augustinian concept of the city of God and the city of Satan. Bishop Pla's letter warned that the Spanish conflict was the prelude to a 'universal conflict in every country of the earth'. 'It takes the external form of a civil war,' he continued, 'but in reality it is a crusade.'[2] With few exceptions, the clergy, the religious orders and the Catholic lay organizations had supported the anti-Republican cause virtually from 1931 onwards. Bishop Pla's letter now placed the seal of Church hierarchy approval on that cause and, by extension, on anything which might be done in its name. Thereafter, the term 'crusade' was not only used repeatedly by members of the national and international Catholic communities to refer to the war but also entered the general vocabulary used by the Nationalists to legitimate the liquidation of the Republic.

In the days prior to the Toledo defeat, the Republic had suffered a number of setbacks on other fronts. In the north, the Nationalists had taken Irún on 5 September and neighbouring San Sebastian had fallen a week later. By 26 September, the Nationalist 'Navarre Brigades' had advanced westward along the coast to within 60 km of the port and industrial centre of Bilbao, capital of Vizcaya. In the same period, Nationalist aircraft had bombarded villages in the Republican rearguard in Asturias. On the Madrid front, after several weeks of fighting, Nationalist troops had taken the Navafría pass in the Guadarrama mountains. Finally, in the Mediterranean, the island of Ibiza had been recaptured by the rebels on 19 September. All over Spain, the Nationalists were consolidating their military position.

Politically, too, important changes took place in the Nationalist camp during the summer of 1936. The National Defence Committee, created on 24 July 1936, constituted the first *ad hoc* response to the need for a coordinating body. However, by the end of the summer, it was becoming clear that the magnitude, complexity and dispersion of the military operations required the supreme authority of a single, overall commander. For, as the chief of the Nationalist air force wrote of the summer of 1936, 'unity of command [is] indispensable to any military action which aspires to victory'.[3] In addition, because the rebels had failed in July to take over all the existing legislative and administrative structures of the state, the Nationalists were faced with the need to create their own, in order to deal with the social, economic and political problems raised by the conflict and to coordinate the solution of these with the strictly military aspects of the war. The military men were reluctant to commend this task to civilians, determined as they were to retain control over what they considered first and foremost a military operation.

As well as increasing the need for efficient military coordination, the prolongation of the conflict and the large scale of the operations also made necessary continual supplies of arms, ammunition and fuel. With most of the country's mining and manufacturing centres in the Republican zone, such supplies had to come mainly from abroad. Since the funds in the Spanish Treasury were also under the control of the legitimate government, the acquisition of these essential materials had to be negotiated in exchange for Spanish raw materials and/or through the concession of financial credits, payable when — and if — the Nationalists won the war. Clearly, foreign governments, financiers and suppliers would need to be convinced that they were dealing with a solid, responsible entity which had both the support of important socio-economic interests and strong possibilities of success, not just with a group generals who seemed to represent nothing more than their own personal and professional dissatisfactions.

The problem facing the Nationalist high command in the late summer of 1936 was thus threefold: how to achieve the optimum conduct of the military aspects of the war; how to manage civilian affairs in the rearguard without parties, politicians or a state administrative apparatus; and how to ensure that the solutions to each of these were mutually compatible. On the initiative of General Kindelán, a meeting was called for 21 September 1936 in Salamanca, to discuss these interrelated questions. It was attended by all of the eleven members of the Defence Committee, plus General Kindelan, as chief of the Nationalist air force. After considerable discussion they approved Kindelan's proposal that one man be commander-in-chief of the Nationalist forces. Then came the question of who that man should be. Apart from considerations of personalities, seniorities and particular ambitions, political sympathies and support would be a key element in making the choice. For the war was the means to a political end, and whoever was chosen as supreme military leader would clearly be in an advantageous position with regard to shaping the political outcome of the conflict. Of those senior officers who might have been candidates at the time of the rising, General Sanjurjo had been killed in an air crash on 20 July, on his way to Spain from his exile in Portugal. General Mola, the 'Director' of the pre-war conspiracy, was not the most senior in rank, while his carlist links and his failure, as Director General of

Security, to support the king in 1931 made him unacceptable to the partisans of the Alfonsist branch of the monarchy. General Cabanellas, the most senior member of the National Defence Committee, was known to have Republican sentiments and was suspected of being a Freemason – hardly desirable characteristics for a leader who would have to nurture good relations with Nazi Germany and Fascist Italy since, in right-wing eyes, Freemasonry was regarded as synonymous with liberalism and leftist subversion. The one man who fulfilled all the requirements of political acceptability and professional capacity was General Francisco Franco. Indeed, his prestige had increased further on the same day that the meeting was held in Salamanca for, as we have seen, it was on that very day that he ordered the detour of his troops to relieve the *alcazar* of Toledo. With the exception of General Cabanellas, who abstained, all those present duly voted for Franco.[4]

When the Defence Committee failed to announce the appointment publicly, Kindelán proposed another meeting to discuss the matter. On 28 September, again in Salamanca, Kindelan proposed to the assembled committee members that the supreme commander of the armed forces should also be head of state for the duration of the war, with responsibility for 'all national activities: political, economic, social, cultural, etc.'[5] When Franco's designation was finally published in the 30 September edition of the Official Bulletin of the National Defence Committee, Franco was referred to as 'head of the Government of the Spanish state' and supreme chief (*generalisimo*) of the Nationalist armed forces.[6] The restriction of the appointment to 'the duration of the war' had been removed. Not content with that, Franco soon began to sign official documents as 'Head of the Spanish state'.

In reality, he had become head of a government and of a state which as yet existed only on paper and in the ambitions of the group most closely associated with him, particularly his elder brother, Nicolás, who acted as his secretary and had assisted Kindelán in drafting his September proposals. Nevertheless, the decree which contained Franco's appointment was no piece of empty word-mongering. It expressed the will that such a state and such a government should exist, in active defiance of the fact that there already existed a constitutional state and a government composed of the democratically elected representatives of the people. On 1 October 1936, Franco took office in Burgos. The following day, the Defence Committee was replaced by a Technical Committee which included some civillians and assumed the role of provisional government in the Nationalist zone. Like the Defence Committee, it was located in Burgos. Franco's military headquarters, however, was now established in Salamanca.

NOTES

1. W. Warlimont, quoted in A. Viñas, *Guerra, dinero, dictadura*, Barcelona, Critica, 1984, p. 59.
2. Quoted in P. Preston *The Spanish Civil War, 1936–39*, London, Weidenfeld & Nicolson, 1990 p. 111.
3. A. Kindelán, *Mis cuadernos de guerra*, Barcelona, Planeta, 1982, p. 102.
4. Ibid. and L. Suarez Fernández, *Francisco Franco y su Tiempo*, vol. II, Madrid, Azor, 1984, p. 100. Neither author reveals for whom Franco himself voted; however, since both state that the decision was unanimous with the exception of Cabanellas, the implication is that Franco voted for himself.
5. Kindelán, op. cit., p. 109.
6. J.P. Fusi, 'Franco, jefe del gobierno' in D. Solar (ed.), *La guerra civil española*, vol. 7, Madrid, Historia 16, 1986–8, p. 90; Kindelán op. cit., p. 110.

5

The Drive For Madrid: October 1936 – May 1937

On the same day that Franco began what was to be a thirty-nine-year term of office, the remains of the legitimate Parliament of the nation met in Madrid. Of the 473 elected members, only 100 were present. They gave full powers to the Prime Minister, Francisco Largo Caballero, and approved a measure which had been under debate, with fierce opposition from the right, at the time of the rising in July: self-government for the Basque Country. To a large extent, this was in recognition of the fact that, in spite of its social and economic affinities with the national parties of the right, the staunchly conservative and Catholic Basque bourgeoisie, represented by the Basque Nationalist Party (*Partido Nacionalista Vasco*, PNV), had remained loyal to the Republican government.[1] The Statute of Autonomy was also granted for practical reasons. The Basque Country was isolated from the rest of Republican Spain by a great swath of rebel-occupied territory. It was extremely difficult, therefore, for the Madrid government to exercise power there, whereas a government acting from Bilbao would be in direct contact with the realities of the situation and should be able to deal with them more effectively. On 7 October 1936, while Nationalist troops closed in on Bilbao, the PNV leader, José Antonio Aguirre, was elected president of Euzkadi (the Basque name for the region) and formed the first autonomous Basque government.

Slowly but surely, the insurgents were also closing in on Madrid from the west and south-west. With the attack from the north halted in the Sierra de Guadarrama and with the east and south-east in Republican hands, Franco's armies increased the pressure on the remaining flank of the capital. On 19 October, Republican forces launched a counter-offensive to the south of Madrid, around the villages of Illescas, Seseña and Esquivias. Their courage and desperation, however, could not make up for their lack of experience and arms, and they were defeated after a few days, suffering heavy losses in the process. They had inflicted considerable damage on the Nationalists, but the latter were spurred on by the scent of victory and bolstered by help from outside, such as the planes sent by Germany and Italy, which, on 24 October, won an aerial battle over Madrid. Four days later, Russian planes bought by the Republic appeared in the capital's skies for the first time, but they could not halt the Nationalist advance, as Franco's troops pressed relentlessly on through the villages on the outskirts of Madrid. By 13 November, the column which had relieved Toledo had reached a large area of parkland on the south bank of the city's river, known as the Casa de Campo. Once a royal hunting forest, its rolling terrain provided an excellent vantage point for artillery attacks on the city. The prime target was the tallest building on the horizon, the central telephone exchange. If the Nationalists put it out of action, Madrid's isolation would be greatly increased, not only because it was at the centre of the capital's telecommunications network but also because it was from there that foreign press correspondents in Madrid sent home their reports on the progress of the war. Franco's forces did not, in fact, manage to destroy the telephone building, but by mid-November, they had crossed the river and made serious inroads into the area occupied by the university campus on the western fringes of the city. In view of the threat of the imminent occupation of Madrid by Francoist troops, the President of the Republic, Manuel Azaña, left the city on 19 October, installing himself in Barcelona.

By this stage, significant changes had taken place in the national and international look of the political map on both

57

sides. In the Nationalist camp, the creation of an incipient 'New State' was beginning to have the desired effect of inspiring in foreign governments confidence which might be translated into material aid. In September, Uruguay had broken off diplomatic relations with the Republic. Portugal followed suit on 23 October, while Guatemala and El Salvador officially recognized Franco as Spanish head of state on 8 November. Ten days later, Franco received important political backing in the form of official recognition by Germany and Italy.

The Republican government, by contrast, received no such declarations of political support from foreign governments. At best, Mexico sent several thousands guns and cartridges in September 1936, and for the time being, the Soviet Union was prepared to supply arms, munitions and foodstuffs. However, its objective in providing this aid was not exclusively, or even primarily, to secure a Republican victory, but to use its intervention in the Spanish war to achieve a collective security agreement with the Western democracies. In any case, Soviet help was not indefinitely guaranteed, nor was it given without a price to be paid. In the first place, the USSR had signed the international agreement on non-intervention in August and might, therefore, at any time decide or be obliged strictly to observe its provisions. Secondly, the continuation of Soviet aid was to a large extent conditional upon the maintenance of good relations between the Republican government and Russian diplomatic and military personnel in Spain. This meant that the government's decisions were not taken solely according to Spanish political criteria but were constrained by considerations of what was convenient to Soviet defence policy. Finally, Soviet aid was not given free of financial charge. To pay for it, the Republic had to use most of the gold and silver reserves held in the Bank of Spain — a transaction which Nationalist propaganda never tired of presenting as nothing short of a robbery perpetrated by the USSR and carried out by the Republican government.

Even where there were no direct political strings attached, the Republic did not find the whole-hearted support it might have expected to receive from fellow-democracies. On 22

November, the British Foreign Secretary, Anthony Eden, managed to persuade his cabinet colleagues not to grant belligerent's rights to Franco, which would have enabled Nationalist warships to stop and search British ships for arms which might be going to the Republic. Nevertheless, it was agreed that the British navy would not protect any British ship suspected by the Francoists of carrying arms to the Republic. This posture reflected the British government's reluctance to become involved in what they saw as an anarchic political situation in Spain and their fears that a Republican victory might have, as one of its consequences, the nationalization or expropriation of British economic interests in Spain.

In the first week of November, events took an unexpected turn. On 4 November, four members of the anarchist CNT joined Largo Caballero's cabinet, thereby sacrificing their ideological rejection of the instruments of state power in the interests of achieving maximum political unity in order to meet the military crisis. Then, in the early hours of 6 November, the Republican government, together with many top-ranking members of the administration, left the beleaguered city of Madrid. They went to Valencia, on the east coast, far from any battle front and still free from maritime blockade. This move had, in fact, been under secret discussion for some weeks, and the reasoning behind it was that, even if Madrid fell, the legitimate government would still be able to carry on the resistance. To many people, however, (including some members of the Cabinet) the sudden and surreptitious departure of the Republic's leaders looked very much like the rats leaving the sinking ship. In the light of this development, the inclusion of the CNT in the government took on an added significance, for it meant that the anarchists bore part of the responsibility for the evacuation. It also ensured that the cabinet and their officials could pass safely through the many road-blocks and checkpoints set up by anarchist militias along the roads out of Madrid.

The Prime Minister, Largo Caballero, was among those who thought that the fall of Madrid was imminent. Nevertheless, he gave orders for the defence of the city to be organized by Generals Miaja and Pozas. The former was to set up a Committee for the Defence of Madrid, composed of representatives of all the political forces present in the Popular Front. With the exception of Miaja himself, none of the committee members was of high rank and most had very limited political or military experience, which hardly augured well for the city's chances of survival. Moreover, the committee was shot through with the same internal political animosities which afflicted the whole of the Republican camp. Thus, the support given by the PCE to the committee and, in particular, to General Miaja was viewed with suspicion by some of the party's adversaries. Yet the committee undoubtedly needed that backing and the Soviet aid to which it was the key. Without them, the Defence Committee could not have staged the city's resistance. There was also another element which played a decisive role in the defence of the capital: the people of Madrid, the *madrileños*. The populace as a whole staged a truly heroic rearguard action. So determined were their efforts that although Nationalist troops were no more than five kilometres from the city centre in November 1936, they were unable to advance any further in the next two and a half years. Indeed, they did not enter the city until the war was declared over, at the end of March 1939. Urged to resist at all costs by the propaganda of the left and party leaders such as the indefatigable communist, Dolores Ibarruri, the inhabitants of Madrid suffered repeated aerial and artillery bombardment, dug trenches, queued for hours for food and fuel, and spent night after night in makeshift beds in the underground railway stations. They worked to provide munitions and clothing for the men at the front, evacuated their children — often with no certainty of ever seeing them again — saw their houses and belongings destroyed by fire and shelling, and ran soup kitchens and shelters for the destitute. Above all, they maintained a tremendous moral integrity in spite of the ever-present threat of defeat and the constant pressure of privation, fear and death.

There were, of course, exceptions and excesses. Not everyone in Madrid was Republican, and as had happened all over the country, those who were caught on the 'wrong' side when war broke out became fugitives, in constant fear of their lives.

Many took refuge in foreign embassies, either until the Red Cross could evacuate them or for the duration of hostilities. Some, like General Franco's brother-in-law, Ramón Serrano Suñer, managed to escape to the Nationalist zone. Others, like the members of the clandestine Falange, engaged in secret anti-Republican activities, hiding fugitives, visiting imprisoned comrades, gathering information and passing it across the enemy lines. Many were imprisoned. Of these, a few were exchanged for Republicans held in Nationalist prisons. Many were shot in the mass executions which took place in October and November 1936 and which the Republican government was apparently unable to prevent. These killings were a grave political mistake as well as an atrocious act of reprisal, for they lent credence to the fears of those who suspected that the Republic had lost control of its own forces and strengthened the Nationalists' claim that they had been forced to rise to 'save' Spain from a barbaric regime.

The battle for Madrid was the first test of the efficacy of a programme of reorganization initiated in the Republican armed forces in the autumn of 1936. Largo Caballero, who was Minister of War as well as head of government, was convinced that only well organized, well disciplined, fully militarized troops could offer effective resistance to the professional soldiers of the Nationalist armies. His conviction was shared by all the other parties of the Republican camp, with the exception of the purist wing of the libertarian movement, who believed that the war would only be won if the social revolution, of which the popular militias were a part, were fully effected. The opinion of the majority prevailed, however, not least because all-important Russian aid was conditional upon the adoption of policies approved by the PCE. On 16 October 1936, Largo Caballero issued a decree whereby the militias and the regular army were amalgamated into one militarized body: the Popular Army. Largo assumed supreme command of the Republican armed forces. He was, in a sense, the Republican *generalísimo*, with the important differences that Largo did not take operational command of the Republican troops, that he had no military experience, and that the Republican camp did not have the structural homogeneity which enabled the Nationalists to establish effective political and military unity of command ('*mando único*').

The basic unit of the Popular Army (which was not fully reorganized until early 1937) was the self-sufficient 'mixed brigade', usually led by regular army officers. As a complementary measure, a body of political commissars was created in October 1936, charged (among other duties) with assisting the military commanders in the task of making the militia volunteers conscious of the importance of rigid discipline. The commissars also carried out a wide variety of other functions, from giving ideological classes to sorting out personal problems. The Nationalists referred to them as 'red chaplains', and the name was not inappropriate. Although, in theory, the commissariat was open to people of all political persuasions, in practice it was staffed mainly by communists. Through its commissars, the PCE exercised considerable influence on the organization and morale of the Popular Army and, therefore, on the military and political conduct of the Republican war effort.

Between 8 and 13 November 1936, the Republican troops manning the trenches on the Madrid front were reinforced by the arrival of the 11th and 12th International Brigades. The decision to create an international volunteer force to fight in Spain had been taken by the executive committee of the Comintern in September, although individual European communist parties has been discussing the idea since the war began. At first, the Republican government had reacted coolly to the proposal but finally assented in view of the critical situation reached by the autumn of 1936. Recruiting took place all over Europe and in the United States, through local branches of each country's communist party, although not all of the volunteers were communists. A clearing office in Paris channelled the volunteers southwards. Over the two years of their participation in the Republican army, between 50,000 and 60,000 Brigaders went to Spain from more than 50 countries. Their presence on the Madrid front in November 1936 undoubtedly provided a vital input of moral as well as military support, although some of the Brigaders themselves were sceptical about their usefulness. 'They didn't need *us*' commented a member of the North American 'Abraham Lincoln' Battalion many years later, 'they needed arms.'[2] Certainly, arms and munitions were in short supply, and it is difficult to assess with accuracy to what extent the International Brigades were essential to the salvation of Madrid. Nevertheless, at a time when non-intervention had isolated the Republic from the rest of the democratic world, the presence of the International Brigaders gave a tremendous boost to Republican morale. In the final analysis, the fact remains that Madrid resisted, and consequently, the war was prolonged.

The fronts established during the autumn remained more or less stable throughout the final weeks of 1936. In the north, the difficulties already experienced by the territory still in Republican hands were increased by the blockading of the ports with mines and patrolling Nationalist ships, but the overland advance of Nationalist troops was halted for the moment. On the Madrid front, Nationalist forces managed to push forward on the main Madrid–Galicia road in the first week of January but were still unable to take the city. By 16 January, a stalemate had been reached, and the front line on the north side of the city remained unchanged until the end of the war in 1939.

In the south, on 22 December, 3,000 Italian 'volunteers' disembarked in Cadiz, followed by a second contingent of 3,000 on 15 January 1937. Meanwhile, the Nationalists advanced eastwards along the Mediterranean coast towards Malaga. During the following week, the coastal villages of San Pedro de Alcántara and Marbella were occupied by Nationalist forces while, in the neighbouring province of Granada, the rebel troops pushed the front some 35 km eastwards. Málaga fell on 8 February 1937. The city was occupied by 20,000 Spanish, Italian and Moroccan troops led by General Queipo de LLano. The Nationalists had won a relatively easy victory, for the Republican defences were weak and the defenders of the city, mostly anarchist militiamen, panicked at the sight of tanks. Hundreds of civilians left the city and were attacked both from the air and by German warships as they fled. As for those who remained, military courts subjected hundreds of prisoners to summary trials before sending them to the firing squad. The repression was so terrible that the Italian ambassador protested to Franco that the Nationalist cause in general and the Italian army in particular were being discredited in foreign eyes. It was, without doubt, the most brutal since Badajoz but, as on that occasion, Franco remained impervious to what foreign public opinion might think of his methods.

While the Nationalists pressed forward in the south and the northern fronts remained in a state of uneasy stalemate, a crucial battle unfolded in the centre in early 1937. For the Nationalists, the Jarama Valley campaign was part of an attempt to sever the main Madrid–Valencia road, which linked the capital to the seat of government. For the Republicans, it was an operation to relieve the pressure on Madrid. A Nationalist force of some 40,000 men began the offensive on 5 February 1937. By 11 February, a unit of Moroccan soldiers had reached the opposite bank of the Jarama River, to be joined by two more Nationalist brigades in the following three days. Both sides fought with tremendous tenacity, and the numbers of casualties were appalling. In the eighteen days that the battle lasted, about 16,000 men were killed. In a single day, the British battalion fighting with the International Brigades lost 400 of its 600 members. There were so many dead and wounded that the legend arose that the Jarama River ran red, not with the earth it carried along with its spring flood but with the blood of soldiers fallen in battle. To add to the tragedy, the battle ended, on 23 February 1937, without a victory for either side.

A week after this inconclusive finale, before the Republicans had had time to recover either their moral or their physical strength, the Nationalist high command launched a new offensive against Madrid, this time to the east of the capital, in the area of Guadalajara. On 8 and 9 March 1937, the rebel army advanced over a front 30 km long and 20 km deep. In this battle, the Italians had been assigned an important role. Three units of the fascist volunteers and one division of the regular

Italian army were to meet at Alcalá de Henares with the troops commanded by two Spanish generals, thus completing the Nationalist encirclement of Madrid. The Italian advance began on 8 March, but the Spanish generals were held up by bad weather. The delay was brief but sufficient to enable the Republican Chief of the General Staff, Colonel Rojo, to deploy three of his best divisions. As the Italians advanced on 10 March, they came across a unit of Italian International Brigaders, the 'Garibaldi Brigade'. Caught off guard by this encounter with compatriots, whom they mistakenly took to be part of their own forces, the fascists were obliged to surrender. Thereafter, the Italians failed to consolidate their advance, and by 14 March they were in full retreat. Heartened by this success, the Republicans passed to the offensive. Bringing all their artillery into play, they broke the Nationalist lines and routed the Italians, who by 22 March, had retreated to a distance of 100 km from Madrid. Once again, and against all odds, the immediate threat to the capital had been averted.

It was unfortunate indeed that Mussolini's crack troops should have suffered such an ignominious defeat precisely at that time, for the new Italian ambassador to Franco's Spain, Roberto Cantalupo, had officially presented his credentials to Franco only two weeks earlier. Moreover, on 2 March, the Fascist Grand Council had expressed its 'solidarity with Nationalist Spain'. The Guadalajara debacle made the diplomatic gestures look like little more than empty rhetoric. On 3 March 1937, the newly appointed German ambassador, von Faupel, also presented his credentials. Thus, to add to the Italians' discomfiture, German diplomacy had a ringside seat to witness Italian military inadequacy. German armed forces, by contrast, were soon to demonstrate their devastating efficiency, in the aerial bombardment of civilian targets.

At the end of January 1937, the original leader of the conspiracy and chief of the Army of the North, General Mola, announced the beginning of a fresh offensive on the Vizcaya front. This was to be the first part of an all-out attempt to take Vizcaya and the adjoining provinces of Santander, Gijón and Oviedo, thus placing the whole of northern Spain in Nationalist hands. Most importantly, it would deprive the Republic of its maritime communications through the ports of Bilbao and Santander, and of the human and economic resources available in the agricultural, mining and industrial areas of the Cantabrian coast. Mola had at his disposal some 18,000 men, divided into four brigades — the 'Navarre Brigades' — and a mixed force of Spanish soldiers led by Italian officers. With these, and support from the air, he believed that the defeat of his adversaries would be rapid, given that, in the Nationalist view, they were militarily inferior to begin with and weakened further by political divisions.

Because of the isolated situation of the Vizcaya front, reinforcements could not be sent to it from other Republican-held areas. The Republican strategy, therefore, was to carry out a surprise attack in some other place, in the hope of distracting Nationalist attention away from Vizcaya. General Solchaga began the Nationalist offensive on 31 March 1937 but was hampered at first by very wet weather, by the mountainous terrain to be crossed, and by the lines of fortifications built around Bilbao, known as the 'Iron Belt'. On the seaward side, Franco announced on 6 April that the northern ports would be blockaded, to prevent supplies from reaching the Republicans. The British Admiralty ordered all British merchant ships within 100 miles of Bilbao to put into the French port of Saint Jean de Luz, and the Prime Minister, Stanley Baldwin, stated in the House of Commons that the British navy would not protect merchant ships which tried to enter Bilbao with food for the Republic. A heated debate ensued and the Leader of the Opposition, Clement Attlee, presented a motion of censure against the Conservative government. Despite the official prohibition, the blockade was in fact broken by a British ship, the *Seven Seas Spray*, which set out from Saint Jean de Luz on 19 April and reached Bilbao with a cargo of anxiously awaited foodstuffs on the following day. Although the supplies were desperately needed, the boost which the show of British solidarity gave to the spirits of the inhabitants of Bilbao was equally important in enabling them to sustain the defence of their city.

Throughout April 1937, the Nationalists pushed towards

Bilbao from the east and south-east. In spite of the weather, the 'Iron Belt', the resistance put up by the Basques and the decoy operations mounted by the Republicans on various other fronts, the towns and villages of Vizcaya fell one by one to the rebels. Gorbea, San Adrian, Urumendi, Urquiola, Barazar, Vergara, Elorrio and Eibar were all occupied between 1 and 26 April. Yet, by then, the campaign had lasted longer than the three weeks many of the Nationalist leaders had anticipated. Perhaps because it was not proving to be the walk-over they had expected, the offensive against Bilbao underwent a qualitative and quantitative change on 26 April. On that day, forces from the German 'Condor Legion' bombed the small town of Guernica during several hours, in one of the most appalling episodes of the entire civil war.

In military terms, Guernica was of strategic interest because it had an arms factory and was a communications centre. Yet the bombardment hit neither the factory nor the key bridge which Republican troops retreating westwards towards Bilbao would have to cross. Within the context of the desire to end the Vizcaya campaign rapidly, there were two motives behind the decision to bomb Guernica. In the first place, Guernica was the cradle of Basque nationalism. It was here that the original Basque parliament building stood, with the sacred oak tree of the Basques alongside. A direct attack on the symbolic roots of Basque nationalism was likely seriously to undermine the morale of the Basque combattants. This was carefully calculated not to cause the opposite effect, however, for neither the parliament building nor the tree were hit. In the second place, Guernica was used as a testing ground for *Blitzkrieg* methods. Again, what was sought was the psychological as much as, or possibly even more than, the material devastation of the civilian population.

The German bombers achieved both objectives to the full. When they finally departed, the centre of Guernica was nothing more than a heap of smouldering rubble, under which lay hundreds of dead and wounded. Those who had escaped the explosive and fire bombs and the machine-gun strafing were numbed by the shock of what had happened, horrified by the frenzied brutality of the attack. Not surprisingly, three days later, the 4th Navarre Brigade was able to occupy without difficulty what remained of Guernica. The Spanish painter, Pablo Ruiz Picasso, learned of the destruction of Guernica while working on a canvas on the subject of the civil war. It had been commissioned by the Republican government for the Spanish pavilion at the Universal Exhibition to be held in Paris that year. In homage to the stricken Basque town, Picasso entitled the finished work, a painting full of the horror and suffering of war, *Guernica*.

Did the attack on Guernica take place with the knowledge and acquiescence of the Nationalist supreme commander, General Franco? At the time, Franco's supporters denied that Guernica had been bombed at all. The official explanation was that the town had been dynamited by retreating Basque troops as part of a 'scorched earth' strategy. Later, the Nationalists admitted that the Condor Legion had destroyed Guernica, but they were careful to stress that it had done so on its own initiative, without the Caudillo's knowledge. This, in fact, was tantamount to saying that, despite Franco's position as supreme military and political authority, the armed representatives of a foreign power could act with complete autonomy in his state. Given Franco's obsession with exercising complete and sole control in the Nationalist zone, it seems inconceivable that this should be true. The available evidence points to the certainty that 'the bombing was undertaken at the request of the Nationalist high command in order to destroy Basque morale and preclude the defence of Bilbao'.[3]

Despite the moral and military blow delivered by the destruction of Guernica, the Nationalist advance in the north was subsequently slowed down. Stormy weather played its part in this, but mostly it was due to the reorganization of the Republican defence and the arrival of a consignment of Czech guns and planes at the beginning of June 1937. The death of General Mola in a bizarre air crash on 3 June was a further setback for the Nationalists, but by then, the die was irreversibly cast in Vizcaya. With General Dávila in Mola's place, the 'Iron Belt' around Bilbao was broken on 12 June, and in a repetition of what had happened in Madrid the previous November, the Basque regional government abandoned Bilbao on 17 June, leaving a Defence Committee in its place. Unlike the *madrileños*, however, the people of Bilbao did not have the resources for prolonged resistance, and Dávila's forces entered the city on 19 June 1937. By the end of the month, the Nationalists had reached the border of Vizcaya and the next province, Santander. The campaign in the north was all but over.

While the military aspects of the war had provided General Franco with nothing but satisfaction in the first half of 1937, the other facet of his dual leadership, as Head of State, was more problematic. As a man with no political experience whatsoever and a firm belief that, in any case, politics were of secondary importance by comparison to military matters, he seems to have given little thought to questions relating to civilian organization, beyond the 'cleansing operations' undertaken to keep his expanding rearguard under control. In the autumn of 1936, however, the resistance of Madrid and the arrival of foreign aid for the Republic made a rapid Nationalist victory far less certain than it had previously seemed. That, in turn, obliged Franco to pay some attention to the possible political effects of a protracted conflict. For, the longer the war continued, the greater was the need to ensure unanimous support and the greater the risk of internal dissent.

The parties which had supported the military rising as the only way to safeguard the socio-economic values and interests of which they were the political representatives had as their common denominator their desire to oust the Popular Front from power. Beyond that, however, their goals were diverse and sometimes even incompatible with each other. The Alfonsist monarchists, the Carlists, the Falangists and the conservatives of the CEDA were agreed that military intervention was necessary, but they were not agreed as to what kind of regime should follow. When the coup turned to war and then the supreme military authority also assumed supreme civilian command, in October 1936, a serious question mark was placed over the post-war role of the civilian social and political forces. Not that the right-wing parties openly dissented from the concentration of state power in the *Generalísimo*. He was, after all, the undisputed hero of a conflict which they supported. It was, rather, that they were concerned lest power in post-war Spain should not be returned to their hands. In order to prevent this from happening, they knew that they must try to maintain a political identity and presence while the war lasted. This expressed itself, not in opposition to Franco, but as a desire to establish a certain autonomy from the military head-quarters and from the provisional − military − government, the Technical Committee.

At the same time, each party tried to maintain elements which differentiated it from the others. Thus, although Falange, Comunión Tradicionalista, CEDA, and Renovación Española members volunteered *en masse* for the Nationalist army on 18 July 1936, they did so not as individuals enlisting in the armed forces but as organized party militias, with their own hierarchy, offering armed support to the regular army. As such, they retained their own uniforms, badges, flags and internal cohesion and, as volunteers, were subject to civilian law. They also maintained their own press and propaganda departments, and their pre-war political structures continued to exist in the Nationalist rearguard. The two largest parties were the Falange and the Carlist Comunión Tradicionalista. This was paradoxical at first sight, for these two had been minority groups before the war. However, with parliamentary politics abolished and party activities severely restricted, the only remaining channel for political activism was through paramilitary action. In this sphere, the Falangists and the Carlists had clear advantages over the other political groups, because their internal organization, style and values were consciously modelled on military lines. Indeed, they conceived of life itself as military service. The new-found strength of the Falange and the Carlists lay in the fact that so many former supporters of parliamentarist credos had abandoned these in favour of the greater 'efficiency' (i.e. greater capacity physically to eliminate opponents) promised by the physical violence of these paramilitary organizations.

In the first months of the war, there was no suggestion that either the Falange or the Comunión Tradicionalista was anything other than totally loyal to Franco. Nevertheless, there existed a continual undercurrent of tension, or of mutual distrust. Franco could not afford to lose the manpower provided by the party militias, which constituted about 35 per cent of the Nationalist army, but he liked barrack-room obedience and wanted no competitors to his one-man rule. Militarily, his supremacy was unquestioned. Politically, although he appeared to stand alone, he was head of an as yet only embryonic, illegal state and did not have effective control of the political forces which would make it into a juridical reality. Certainly, Franco had the advantage that all the pre-war political leaders had either died or been discredited. Even so, there were people in the lower ranks of the Falange and the Comunión capable of drumming up their own support and of reinforcing it with their militiamen. Consequently, in the autumn of 1936, at the instigation of his brother, Nicolás, Franco began to consider ways of achieving complete control of the political forces in his camp. The first idea was that he should form his own party; this was rejected, probably because it was too reminiscent of the failure of the dictator Primo de Rivera's attempt to create a party, the *Unión Patriótica* (Patriotic Union). The next proposal was the amalgamation of all the existing parties into one, with Franco as its leader. The state created by the force of arms would thus acquire a civilian structure through which to shape the ideological justification of the war and to absorb, by a mixture of coercion and co-option, the political forces which, otherwise, would remain as mere external collaborators in a military rising. By making them co-partners in the construction of the 'New State', but under his control and authority, Franco proposed to pre-empt any possible notions of dispensing with him once the war was over.

The first step in the plan to divest the Nationalist political forces of any autonomous power was a decree issued in December 1936, whereby the party volunteers at the front would be subject, not to civilian or party, but army discipline, while those in the rearguard would answer to the Civil Guard, itself a paramilitary force. In addition, although existing militia units were to maintain their identity, new recruits would be

71

incorporated into the regular army, according to normal re-cruitment procedures. Equally, casualties in the militias would be replaced from the regular army, but these men would not necessarily be party members. The result of these measures was that party recruits were now distributed throughout the armed forces, and it would be difficult in the future for any one group to back up political initiatives with armed action. In this way, the Nationalist political organizations would be unable to jeopardize Franco's primary objective: winning the war.

This was as far as Franco's politico-military measures went for the moment, which suggests that he considered the question of the structure of the 'New State' a long-term matter. There was, however, one person in Franco's camp who was concerned that the political organization of the Nationalist zone should be undertaken at once, not when the war was over. Ramón Serrano Suñer had reached Franco's headquarters in Salamanca in February 1937. He was not a military man but a lawyer and former rightist member of parliament for Zaragoza. He was also married to the younger sister of Franco's wife and was, therefore, linked to the *generalísimo* by close family ties. An astute political analyst with a deep-seated loathing of the Re-public, which he held responsible for the death of his two brothers in war-torn Madrid, Serrano was immediately incor-porated into Franco's team of collaborators. According to his own account of this period, he was profoundly impressed by the need to provide some kind of formal structure through which to unite and articulate political support for the Nationalist war effort. Although he has always denied that he played a fundamental role in the creation of such a structure, the truth is that, from February 1937 onwards, rearguard political activity intensified noticeably, and the rumour began to circulate that a totalitarian system was being planned, in which political rep-resentation would be through a single party, to be created by fusing all the existing parties together.

Since Franco had already been proclaimed head of the armed forces, of the government and of the state, it was a foregone conclusion that, should the idea of the single party become reality, he would also assume the leadership of the party. A jockeying for positions now began among the different political groups, which clearly indicated that, notwithstanding their common interest in the victory of the Nationalist cause, they were reluctant to renounce their particular party and personal interests in the process. An internal crisis began to brew in the Nationalist camp, of which the leading players were the Falangists and the Carlists. In addition, antagonistic factions emerged within each of these parties, while all were increasingly conditioned by the feeling that a 'solution' to their differences might be imposed on them by the *generalísimo*. No one seemed to question the principle of a single party, but for some Falangists and Carlists the crucial issue was that its national leader should be one of their own number, elected by them from within their own ranks. For others, the important thing was to achieve a stronger position from which to bargain by uniting spontaneously before Franco made their union obligatory.

The crisis reached a climax in mid-April 1937. In the absence of its founder and national chief, Primo de Rivera, and with many of its provincial leaders dead, in prison or in hiding in the Republican zone, Falange Española de las JONS had created a provisional governing body in August 1936, which was chaired by the party boss in the province of Santander, Manuel Hedilla. A meeting of the Falangist National Council was called for 18 and 19 April, in Salamanca, to discuss the question of the party leadership. By then it was known that Primo de Rivera had been executed in a Republican jail on 20 November 1936, and the Falangists were anxious to appoint a permanent replacement. On the night of 16 April, in an incident which has never been entirely clarified, rival Falangist factions clashed in Salamanca, causing the death of two of their number. The Council meeting began on 18 April in an atmosphere of great tension. After a day of heated, often acrimonious discussion, Hedilla was elected national chief by a narrow margin of votes. Franco, however, was not the man to allow conflict in the rearguard to endanger the unity of the Nationalist war effort and, therefore, jeopardize the possibilities of victory. On 19 April 1937, he issued a decree which amalgamated the Falange and the Carlist Com-

73

unión Tradicionalista, under the new title of Falange Española Tradicionalista y de las JONS (FET y de las JONS). All the other parties of the right were automatically dissolved and their members incorporated into FET y de las JONS. The leader of this hybrid was, of course, General Franco.

The long-term importance of the Decree of Unification, as it was immediately baptized, was that it laid the foundation stone of a political system which subsequently remained in force for almost forty years. Political parties, competitive elections by secret ballot, universal suffrage, freedom of speech and propaganda and, above all, the right to dissent all remained proscribed until 1976, when Franco had been dead for over a year. In the short term, the Unification nipped in the bud a serious outbreak of internal conflict and left Franco without any effective political rivals. It also revealed that, in a tug of water between military and civil powers, the former had the whip hand. When, in the aftermath of Franco's political masterstroke, Manuel Hedilla and a number of other Falangists protested against the terms of the Unification, they were immediately arrested, tried and given harsh sentences. Indeed, Hedilla was only saved from execution by the intervention on his behalf of the German Ambassador to Salamanca, von Faupel. His imprisonment and disgrace were, as Franco intended, a cautionary tale for anyone who might entertain ideas of doing anything other than accepting without question Franco's dictates.

NOTES

1. One other Catholic party remained loyal to the Republic: the Catalan *Unió Democràtica* (Democratic Union).
2. William Susman, interview with S. Ellwood in D. Solar (ed.), *La guerra civil española*, vol. 8, Madrid, Historia 16, 1986−8.
3. P. Preston, *The Spanish Civil War, 1936−39*, London, Weidenfeld & Nicolson, 1990, p. 142.

6

The Republic's Desperate Struggle:
May 1937 — April 1938

At about the same time as the April crisis broke in the Nationalist zone, a similar situation arose in the Republican rear-guard.
Although more complex in character, it, too, was the fruit of
competition for hegemony and of divergent concepts of what
kind of political system the war was being fought to achieve.
However, whereas Franco resolved the Nationalist crisis by
subjugating the power of the rightist political forces to his own,
imposing unity upon them and making their existence dependent
on his will, the Republican leadership was unable to hold its
political support together or to assert itself in such a way as
to override the divisions which existed between parties and
individuals. In part, this was because the Republican government's commitment to democratic practices prevented it from
applying the kind of authoritarian tactics which were second
nature to Franco and his henchmen. To an important degree,
it was also due to the fact that the Republic's dependence on
Soviet aid reduced the political autonomy of the decision-
makers and increased the PCE's capacity to influence the
course of events. The tragic net result was that, whereas the
autocratic Franco emerged fortified from his crisis, the democratic Republic was seriously debilitated by the way it resolved
its own.

Since the turn of the century, Barcelona had been the great
stronghold of anarchist militancy. There, too, the anti-Stalinist

POUM had its largest following. When the military rising had been defeated in July 1936, the government of Catalonia found its authority superceded by the Central Committee of Anti-Fascist Militias, created on 21 July as the executive organ of popular power and dominated by the anarchists of the CNT and their semi-secret extremist organization, the FAI. In an attempt to reassert the rule of law and to unite all the Catalan forces loyal to the Republic, the President, LLuis Companys, dissolved the Militias Committee on 26 September 1936 and formed a new regional government with representatives from all the parties of the left and centre, including the Catalan communist party (Partit Socialist Unificat de Catalunya, PSUC; Unified Socialist Party of Catalonia), the POUM and the CNT. In a similar attempt to achieve maximum unity, as we have noted earlier, four anarchists were incorporated into the central Republican cabinet on 4 November 1936. However, it was naive to imagine, even in the context of a civil war, that giving people governmental responsibility and representation would dissolve ideological differences and personal animosities which had existed between them for decades. The PCE criticized Largo Caballero's handling of military affairs and called for the dissolution of its rival, the POUM, while, on 27 March 1937, the anarchist representatives resigned from the Catalan government because it had decreed that all arms seized by civilians in July 1936 must be surrendered. Companys formed yet another cabinet on 16 April, which again included the anarchists, but the price of their participation was the cancellation of the order to hand over arms. With that crisis barely resolved, a fresh one broke when the anarchists accused the communists of running their own 'private' prisons on the margins of the state prison system. Tension reached breaking point on 25 April, when the death of a well-known communist was attributed to anarchist assassins. On the same day, a clash between anarchists and members of the Republican frontier police (the *Carabineros*) heralded the outbreak of serious fighting.

Between 3 and 7 May 1937, the centre of Barcelona was the scene of fierce fighting between anarchists and POUMists on the one hand and communists, socialists and left Republicans on the other. The English writer, George Orwell, on his way to join the 'Abraham Lincoln Battalion' of the International Brigades, was then in Barcelona and later described the events of May 1937 in *Homage to Catalonia*. President Companys and leaders of the anarchist CNT and socialist UGT publicly called for an end to the fighting and to the general strike which accompanied it, but it was not until a large contingent of Assault Guards was sent in by the government in Valencia that the revolt began to subside, on 8 May 1937.

The war-within-the-war in Barcelona had ended, but the deeper crisis of which it was part had not. While the anarchists accused the communists of provoking the Barcelona clash, the communists blamed it on the socialist Interior Minister, Angel Galarza, and demanded that the CNT and the POUM be punished. Prime Minister Largo Caballero refused to give in to their demands, for he was anxious not to allow their influence to increase. Already, in April, he had taken steps to curtail what he considered their excessive power by placing limitations on the authority and functions of the War Commissariat and by dissolving the Madrid Defence Committee. The communist presence in both bodies was undoubtedly very strong, but Largo's view was not shared by all the members of his cabinet. At a meeting held on 13 May, Largo found himself isolated. His only potential supporters were the four anarchist ministers. However, given the tension which existed between Largo's socialists and the CNT, it was unlikely that a lasting alliance could be forged at cabinet level. Largo thought of forming a new government, from which the communists would be excluded. However, as his socialist colleagues Indalecio Prieto and Juan Negrín reminded him, such a move was inconceivable since it would almost certainly put an end to desperately needed Russian aid. On 15 May, President Azaña accepted Largo's resignation and asked Dr Negrín to form a new government. The cabinet he presented on 18 May did not include any anarchists or '*caballerista*' socialists. In June, the anarchists withdrew from the regional government of Catalonia. The POUM, which had already been excluded from the *Generalitat* some time earlier, in December 1936, now suffered the consequences of what was nothing short of a witch-hunt. Its newspaper was prohibited and fifty of its most prominent activists were arrested. The most important of these, Andreu Nín, died in prison on 20 June 1937, almost certainly as a result of being brutally tortured by Stalinist agents.

Given the essential link between ideology and the war in both the Nationalist and Republican camps, it is surprising that the events of Spring 1937 were restricted to the rearguard and did not have serious repercussions in the trenches. In part, this was due to the force and rapidity with which the dissenters were repressed and, in part, to the dynamics of front-line life, where the enemy army was a more immediate and fearful presence than differences of political opinion in one's own camp. Military fortunes were only to a limited degree susceptible to the vicissitudes of political developments, but the reverse was less true. However, whereas Franco's political prestige was continually enhanced by the military progress of the war, that of the Republican leaders continually depreciated as more and more territory fell to the enemy. When the Nationalist armies reached the northern province of Santander at the beginning of July 1937, the Republicans decided to launch a grand offensive on the Madrid front. It was hoped thereby to restore both the authority of the military and political leaders and the flagging morale of troops and civilians. At the same time, the operation was conceived as an attempt to delay the fall of Santander.

On the night of 5 July 1937, General Miaja and Colonel Rojo launched a massive surprise attack on the Nationalist lines around the village of Brunete, 30 km west of Madrid, where the enemy defences were relatively weak. By 12 July, they had broken through the Nationalist lines and had occupied a number of small villages. By then, however, the Nationalists had recovered from their initial confusion and managed to halt the Republican advance. The final outcome of the battle hung in the balance. Typical of its indecisive nature was what happened in the village of Villanueva del Pardillo, which changed hands several times in the course of a single day. By 18 July, the first anniversary of the rising, the Republican forces were on the defensive, and the battle had turned into one of attrition. A week later, the dreaded Moroccan troops entered the now ruined village of Brunete. The Republicans put up desperate resistance, fighting even in the cemetery, but were unable to carry through a counter-attack they launched on 25 July. This was the feast-day of Santiago (St James the Great), patron saint of Spain, and the Nationalists were quick to seize on the coincidence as yet another sign that God and, therefore, Right were on their side. On the following day, fired with the certainty that they had divine assistance, the Nationalists overcame the last pockets of resistance in Brunete and Franco ordered a ceasefire.

The battle of Brunete cost both sides thousands of men. For the Republican military and political leaders, it also meant the demoralization provoked by the failure of a desperate attempt to recover territory, prestige and confidence. To a large extent, this battle was a watershed for the Republic. From that point onwards, the Popular Army was no longer thought of as the instrument for winning the war, but simply as the means to hold out as long as possible. That the war lasted another two years was as much due to the grim tenacity of the Spanish people as to the quality of the Popular Army.

Although sporadic fighting had continued in the north throughout the Brunete offensive, positions did not alter greatly. Had the Republicans achieved a victory at Brunete, the Nationalists might have been sufficiently weakened, militarily and psychologically, to enable the remainder of the northern front to hold out indefinitely. This was not the case, however, and the Nationalist army now prepared to launch a final attack in the north. Fighting was resumed in the province of Santander on 14 August 1937, with the Navarre Brigades and an Italian volunteer force pressing north through the passes of the 'Picos de Europa' mountains. The defending Republican forces were numerous, but their lack of arms and munitions was aggravated by the knowledge that this was a fight to the death and, in all probability, a losing battle. Each day brought a

79

fresh defeat as the Navarre Brigades and the Italian 'Black Arrows' came closer to Santander, in pre-war days a favourite holiday resort for middle-class families anxious to escape the heat of the central plain. By 21 August, the Nationalists were within 20 km of their objective, and five days later, they entered Santander, where they organized a triumphant parade. The final stage of the Santander campaign came on 27 August when, in the village of Santoña, the last eleven battalions of the Republic's Northern Army surrendered to the 'Black Arrows'.

The surrender had been negotiated two days earlier by Basque members of the northern Defence Committee, in the hope of saving the Basque militias from the reprisals which inexorably followed occupation of an area by the Nationalists. The Basques expected that repressive measures against them would be particularly severe, for in the Nationalists' eyes, the leading Basque party — the conservative and very Catholic Basque Nationalist Party — had betrayed its 'natural' social and ideological allies by siding with the Republic. As soon as Bilbao had fallen, in June 1937, Franco's Technical Committee had announced the suspension in Vizcaya and Guipúzcoa of the special economic regime enjoyed until then by the four Basque provinces. Navarre and Alava, by contrast, retained their economic privileges, in recognition of their support for the Nationalist cause. Despite the much-vaunted 'crusading' nature of the rising, the bishop of the Basque diocese of Vitoria had been expelled from Nationalist Spain in October 1936. A group of Basque priests had been executed by a Francoist firing squad in December, on suspicion of supporting the Basque nationalist cause, and as the bombardment of Guernica in April 1937 had shown, the secular populace in Euzkadi was a prime target for Francoist brutality.

It was because they had already seen these examples of the Nationalists' detestation of those whom they regarded as separatists (and, therefore, subversives) that the retreating Basque forces preferred to surrender to the Italians, from whom they hoped to receive more lenient treatment. Sure enough, the Italian who received the Basque surrender promised to respect the lives of the rank-and-file and to allow the officers to embark on boats bound for exile. The Spanish military command had different ideas, however. When Nationalist officers arrived in Santoña on 27 August, they obliged the Basques to disembark and then took them all prisoner. This pitiful episode not only failed to save the remains of the Basque army from reprisals but also served to sharpen the existing divisions within the Republican camp, when it became known that the leaders of the PNV had been prepared to do a deal with the enemy to save their own partisans, regardless of the fact that this meant abandoning other northerners and the Republic as a whole to their fate.

With the fall of Santander, the only northern area left in Republican hands was the rapidly diminishing pocket around Oviedo and Gijón, in Asturias. The Nationalists were anxious to end the northern campaign before the winter set in and launched a well-armed, determined offensive to that end in September. By then, however, the weather had already begun to worsen, and this, together with the mountainous nature of the country in Asturias, made the advance slower and more exhausting than anticipated. Even knowing they were beaten, the Asturian militias resisted to the last ounce of their strength and the last stick of their dynamite, remembering the terrible repression that had followed their abortive revolution in 1934. The Nationalists had the advantage in numbers and arms, however, and the battle for Gijón and Oviedo ended on 21 October 1937. The campaign in the north was finally over, except for the mass arrests, imprisonments and executions of Republican loyalists which inevitably followed.

While the Navarre Brigades and the 'Black Arrows' closed in on Santander in August, the Republican armies revived the conflict on the Aragón front, in an attempt both to isolate and capture Zaragoza and to draw Nationalist forces away from Santander. On 24 August, six Republican units attacked the Nationalist lines along the entire Aragón front, from north of Huesca to south of Zaragoza. They did not, however, have large numbers of well-trained troops nor the experienced officers required by an operation on such a large scale. Consequently, it degenerated into a series of fierce, but unconnected, battles. The longest and hardest of these was that fought in the area around the villages of Belchite and Quinto, some 60 km south-east of Zaragoza, in the valley of one of Spain's largest waterways, the River Ebro. For two weeks, a desperate battle raged in and around Belchite, where a relatively small contingent of Nationalists were under siege in the buildings of a convent, in a situation reminiscent of Toledo. Unlike what had happened to the *alcazar*, however, this siege ended in victory for the Republicans, whose forces entered the shattered ruins of Belchite on 6 September. Despite this minor success, the main object of the offensive, Zaragoza, remained in Nationalist hands.

By the beginning of the winter of 1937, Franco's forces occupied a little more than half of peninsular Spain, plus Spanish Morocco and the Canary and Balearic Islands, except Menorca. The completion of the northern campaign not only gave them an enormous psychological and economic boost, but also provided them with the strategic advantage of being able to concentrate their forces on the two principal remaining fronts: Madrid and Aragón/Catalonia.

The course of the war, almost entirely favourable to Franco, both influenced and was influenced by international responses to events in Spain. Throughout 1937, Franco consolidated his position as, one by one, foreign governments conceded official recognition to the Francoist state. On 2 October, the League of Nations admitted officially that the policy of non-intervention had failed, as the Nationalists openly received men and arms from Portugal, Germany and Italy and the Republicans took delivery of tanks, guns and advisers from the Soviet Union. Defenders of liberty and democracy all over the world volunteered for active service in the Republican lines or collected funds to supply the Republic with vital medicines, foodstuffs and clothing. However, the reality of the balance of power was reflected in the Texas Oil Company's supply of petroleum to the Nationalists, the Vatican blessing of the 'crusade', the British commercial and diplomatic representatives in Burgos and the closing of the French frontier. By the autumn of 1937, no one held out any hope for the survival, let alone the victory, of the Republic. Moreover, the western democracies had been nervous about the instability of the Republic even before the outbreak of war and now feared that to support it would mean strengthening international communism. Faced with that possibility, they opted to abstain from giving the Republic military or political support. In fact, it was precisely that stance which, by leaving a clear field, enabled the communists to tighten their grip on the military and political machinery of Republican Spain.

Activity on both sides of the political divide in late 1937 encouraged external observers to conclude that the end of the war was near. On 1 November 1937, the Republican government transferred its residence again, this time from Valencia to Barcelona, where it was shortly joined by the members of the Basque regional government. Thus, all the governing bodies of the Republic were in the area closest to the French border and the Mediterranean coast. Ordinary people in the Republican zone could scarcely avoid concluding that their leaders were preparing for rapid evacuation. In the Nationalist zone, Franco placed another stone in the nascent edifice of his 'New State' when, on 2 December, the members of its advisory body, the National Council of FET y de las JONS, were sworn in at Burgos. At the same time, one of the few surviving founder members of the 1931 Falange, Raimundo Fernández Cuesta, was appointed Secretary General of the Party – a post whose incumbent was always entirely subservient to the will of General Franco. Militarily, too, the indications were that the war could not last much longer. The Republican General Staff knew that the Nationalists were planning a final assault on Madrid for mid-December. Using a by then familiar (but repeatedly unsuccessful) ploy, they hurriedly prepared an operation on the Aragón front to be put into practice before the attack on Madrid could begin. Mustering as many men and arms as they could, the Republicans attacked the town of Teruel, 180 km south of Zaragoza, on 15 December 1937.

Teruel is situated on the eastern edge of the peninsula's central massif, at an altitude of 915 metres. Its climate is extreme, with hot, dry summers and very cold winters. It began to snow on the day the Republicans launched their attack, and by 17 December, a blizzard had severed communications. Thereafter, it was almost impossible to advance, except on foot and only then with great difficulty. Supplies of food and ammunition were held up by the snow, and the wounded could not be evacuated. The hardships occasioned by the weather were made worse by the fact that many of the Republican troops had come from Belchite and were still only equipped with summer clothing. They had neither boots nor heavy coats to withstand the sub-zero conditions of what turned out to be the most severe winter in decades. Many men lost hands and feet from frostbite, and morale was, understandably, low. Nevertheless, they battled on, and on 21 December, amid machine gun fire and dynamiting from house to house, they entered the outskirts of Teruel.

In response, Franco had decided to suspend the Madrid offensive in order to send reinforcements to Teruel. He did not allow Christmas to stand in his way: by 25 December, his troops had reached the town and had launched their counter-attack, with vital air-cover being provided by the planes of the German 'Condor Legion'. The Nationalist garrison inside the town surrendered on 7 January 1938, and the Republicans then managed to hold on to Teruel during six weeks of incessant bombardment in appalling climatic conditions. By then, they were fighting a purely defensive action, however. When the Nationalists threatened to surround Teruel from the north, the Republicans had not the strength to counter-attack, and the only salvation possible was retreat. On 21 February 1938, the Republican forces abandoned the shattered remains of Teruel, leaving it to be reoccupied by the Nationalists the following day. Once again, the Republic had expended huge amounts of its dwindling human and material resources to no avail. At best, it had succeeded in reducing the pressure on Madrid; at worst, it had cost the Republicans over 60,000 lives and had increased the antagonism between those — including the socialist Defence Minister, Prieto — who were beginning to think the war lost and those who, like the socialist Prime Minister, Negrín, and the communists, rejected this view as 'defeatist'.

Although Franco had interrupted his efforts to take Madrid, the capital remained the ultimate objective, and everyone expected that he would return to it sooner or later. For the moment, he was content to isolate Madrid even further by making a concerted drive on the remaining Republican territory in the east. This had, in fact, begun even before the fall of Teruel. On 5 February 1938, the Nationalist army attacked in the valley of the River Alfambra, to the north of Teruel. Franco took personal command of the operation. By 8 February, the Nationalist troops of General Yagüe had advanced several kilometres, but they were then slowed by snow and rain. The Republicans regrouped and were able to make a brief stand, but their resistance was in vain, and the battle of the Alfambra ended on 8 March 1938 with another victory for the seemingly invincible forces of the *Generalísimo*. Franco now prepared to advance on the remainder of the Aragón front. Some 160,000 men, supported by hundreds of tanks and planes, began the offensive on 7 March 1938.

That same day, the National Council of FET y de las JONS met in Burgos to approve the first piece of Francoist legislation to be drafted with post-war organization in mind. On 30 January 1938, Franco had replaced the eight-man Technical Committee, created in October 1936, with a twelve-man cabinet whose task was to begin the construction of the legislative framework of the post-war state and to give an appearance of constitutional legitimacy to the Nationalist regime. The Francoist legislators started not, as might have been expected, with a general statement of the regime's principles, a declaration of citizens' rights or a policy statement, but with a Labour Charter, modelled on the Italian fascist *Carta del Lavoro* which laid down the ground rules for the social and economic control of the working masses. The choice of topic reflected the pride of place given to the belief that the working classes must be kept strictly in order. The content of the Charter indicated that the Francoist state would be economically corporatist, socially imbued with the values most dear to reactionary conservatism (such as hierarchy, order and authority), and administered by the bodies which incorporated those values, the army and the party. The war was not yet over, but the Nationalists were fully confident that they would be running the show when it was. Naturally, the National Council of FET y de las JONS gave its unanimous approval to the document which enshrined the principles for whose imposition its members and their like were fighting.

By the end of March, the Nationalists had pushed the Aragón front almost 100 km eastwards and had entered Catalonia. Their success was as powerful a weapon against the Republicans as their superiority in men and arms. When it was known that Franco's armies were close to Lérida, on the western edge of Catalonia, the Republican Defence Minister, Indalecio Prieto, expressed the opinion that the time had come to attempt peace negotiations. By then, the Republican army was much depleted in quantity and quality. With the defeat suffered in the north, four army corps had been lost, and since then, losses had been continual on the Aragón front. To replace them, more recruits were called up, but they were progressively younger, sometimes only fifteen or sixteen years old. Consequently, by March 1938, the Popular Army had few veterans, and the lack of experienced officers was exacerbated by the increasingly hasty and inadequate training given to new recruits before despatching them to the front line. In addition to the deficiencies of their human resources, there were also those of their armaments. While Franco continually received fresh supplies from Italy and Germany, the closure of the French border meant that the French and Russian war *matériel* bought by the Republic was either held up in France or had to be transported, at great risk, by sea. Whole shipments of fuel and arms had been lost as a result of enemy action in the Mediterranean.

In such inferior conditions, it was clear that the Republic could not possibly win the war. At best, it could try to hold out in the hope that a general conflict in Europe would oblige the western democracies actively to intervene in support of the Spanish Republic. However, despite Hitler's invasion of Austria on 11 March, appeasement was still the policy of the British government, and although France reopened its border with

Spain, this was a compromise measure, for the French Prime Minister, Blum, had failed to obtain his government's approval for his proposal that France aid the Republic militarily. When, in late March, Prieto suggested seeking peace talks with the Nationalists, he was attacked by the communists, whose anxiety to remove him from the Defence Ministry was scarcely if at all concealed. By then, the Republican cabinet was irreversibly split over the crucial question of what line to follow: resistance or negotiation with the enemy. Even as Yagüe's Moroccan troops entered Lérida on 3 April 1938, yet another crisis arose in the Republican government. Negrín formed a new cabinet two days later, from which Prieto and a fellow socialist, Julián Zugazagoitia, were excluded. They were replaced by socialists who, like Negrín and the Communist Party, felt that the war must go on.

Meanwhile, spurred on by their continual victories, the Nationalist troops pushed eastwards and had little difficulty in overcoming what little resistance they encountered. On 15 April 1938, they reached the Mediterranean coast at a small town called Vinaroz, half-way between Valencia and Barcelona. This was an enormous moral and strategic victory, for it meant that the territory still in Republican hands had been cut in half. Catalonia was now a separate entity in the same way that the occupation of Irún and San Sebastian had isolated the northern provinces. And in the same way that the northern defeat had deprived Madrid of one of its two prime sources of economic and military resources, separation from Catalonia now virtually deprived it of the other, for it was well nigh impossible to transport goods or people from one area to the other. In addition, Barcelona was then the seat of the Republican government. Consequently, the entire centre-south zone, including Madrid, had been cut off not only from vital supplies of food and arms, but also from the political authority of the government. Not surprisingly, the psychological impact of physical isolation had a very negative effect on the morale of the civilian population in the centre-south zone of the Republic. Indeed, this territorial division and the sense of defencelessness it gave the population were key factors in the creation of the climate of desperation and panic in which the Republic's final political crisis was to unfold, a year later.

7

The Third and Final Year: April 1938 – March 1939

In the second half of April 1938, Franco consolidated the Vinaroz victory with the occupation of Tortosa, 50 km to the north, and Peñíscola, 20 km to the south. However, contrary to what Republican observers expected and Nationalist military leaders advised, Franco did not follow this up with an immediate drive on Barcelona. Cautious strategist that he was, he thought that, if he were to move his best troops into the northeast corner of the peninsula and war were then to break out in Europe, he might find himself outflanked by invading French troops. In order to avoid the possibility of being trapped in Catalonia, Franco opted instead for an offensive against Valencia. In so doing, he hoped to cut off the maritime supply route between Barcelona and Valencia, thereby completely isolating Madrid from the remittances of arms and food which still managed to trickle through.

The political situation in both zones was also a factor to be taken into consideration. The resolution of the April 1938 crisis in the Republican cabinet had effectively meant the consolidation of the pro-resistance lobby. This was apparent in a thirteen-point policy declaration published on 1 May 1938, in which the Prime Minister, Negrín, reaffirmed the Republic's position as a legally constituted regime inspired by egalitarian and democratic principles, reiterated Spain's adherence to the ideals of the League of Nations and proposed an end to foreign intervention in Spanish affairs. In fact, the international response to Negrín's call for solidarity with Spanish anti-fascist resistance was nil, but this only became apparent later. At the beginning of May, the Negrín government found itself enjoying a moment of relative (and ephemeral) buoyancy.

In the Nationalist camp, there were indications that, beneath the surface of imposed unity, voices of dissent were murmuring. In the same way that the Republicans were obliged to call up ever-younger recruits, so the Nationalists' initial reliance on the Army of Africa veterans gave way, in time, to the incorporation of men and officers who were not professional soldiers and who were shocked by the horrible reality of war. Even an old hand like Yagüe was concerned by the vast scale of the destruction. On 19 April 1938, the first anniversary of the creation of the 'single party', he made a speech in which he proposed that the Falange should be the channel for the reconciliation of the two sides in conflict. He was immediately disciplined for even suggesting the idea of a negotiated end to the war, for Franco was intent upon total victory and would hear nothing of peace talks or reconciliation. Such was his hatred of the Republic and everything it stood for, and such his all-consuming ambition to be the absolute master of Spain, that he deliberately chose to go on subjecting his fellow citizens to the suffering of war, even when, in military terms, it was virtually impossible for the Republic to recover and turn the tables. Knowing they could expect no peace settlement from Franco, the Republicans rejected the idea of surrender and fought desperately on.

During May, the Nationalists advanced towards the coastal town of Castellón de la Plana, but they had to fight hard for every kilometre of ground they gained from Republican reinforcements sent from the Madrid front. In many villages, the population had set fire to crops and buildings before fleeing, thus diminishing supplies of food and shelter for Franco's armies. The advance on Castellón was also slowed by harrassing actions carried out at the northern end of the front, between Lérida and the Pyrenees. The fighting was particularly fierce around the village of Tremp, for, on 7 April 1938, the

Nationalists had taken control of a huge reservoir and power station there and had cut off part of Catalonia's electricity supply. Republican attempts to recover the area were unsuccessful, but they did at least have a delaying effect on the Nationalist advance. In June, the initiative was taken by the Nationalist air force, consisting of about 1,000 German and Italian planes. Throughout that month, Nationalist aircraft pounded the towns and ports of the east coast. They struck at inland targets, too: the arms manufacturing centre of Sagunto was bombed on 13 June, and a week later, the target was the airfield at Manises, where the Republican air force carried out vital repairs to its dwindling stock of battered planes. On the same day that Sagunto was bombed, the Nationalists occupied Castellón, and the French again closed the frontier with Catalonia. The bombing raids continued throughout July, in a relentless effort to smash what was left of Republican manufacturing and communications infrastructures.

Negrín's appeal to the western democracies had elicited no response, yet he clung to the hope that the Republic could stay alive until a European conflict should save it. He knew, however, that the Republican forces on the east coast could not hold out indefinitely without fresh supplies of arms and men, and that neither commodity was available. Consequently, the Republic resorted, as on previous occasions, to mounting a surprise operation on a different front, with the immediate purpose of detaining Franco's advance on Valencia. The Nationalists were also putting pressure on the Catalan front, which followed the course of two rivers, the Segre and the Ebro, in a long curve from the Pyrenees to the Mediterranean. With the bulk of Franco's forces distributed between the Madrid and Valencia fronts, however, the Catalan front was relatively quiet and thinly manned. In the first half of July, the Republicans began to gather men, planes and arms on the north bank of the Ebro, at a point where the curve of the river left a tongue of Nationalist territory flanked on either side by Republican-held land.

On the night of 24 July 1938, Republican troops began to cross the river in small boats which had been brought overland from the Catalan coast in the preceding weeks. The crossing took the Nationalists completely by surprise, and for about a week, the Republicans had the upper hand. By then, they had managed to transport about 50,000 troops across the river, using what anti-aircraft guns they had to protect the boats and the pontoon bridges they had constructed. Between 24 and 31 July, the Republicans occupied several villages on the south bank of the Ebro, albeit sustaining heavy losses in the process. By the end of the month, however, the Nationalist defence had recovered from its initial surprise. Troops were hastily transferred from the Valencia front, and the Republican advance was halted on 1 August. Conditions were extremely difficult for both sides, with little natural cover available on the scrubby hills and the movement of troops, wounded and supplies possible only under cover of darkness. The Republican strategy had, indeed, delayed the Nationalist advance on Valencia. However, as had happened in December 1937, when the battle of Teruel halted what otherwise might have been the final assault on Madrid, the Ebro campaign now turned into a long, gruelling struggle, in which neither side had much to gain, but the Republicans had the best part of a seriously depleted army to lose. Many of the combattants must have been reminded, too, of Brunete, as they struggled not only against the enemy but also against the heat, dust, sweat and thirst of the height of the Spanish summer.

The battle of the Ebro dragged on until 16 November 1938, when the Republicans were forced back across the river and the lines were re-established where they had been in July. This did not mean, however, that everything was as it had been before the battle. Each side had lost about 40,000 men, but whereas the Republican troops were physically and morally shattered, the Nationalists had experienced the stiffening effect of a set-back, followed by the satisfaction of ultimate victory. In political terms, too, while Franco's star shone ever more brightly, that of Negrín began to wane. Had the Ebro offensive resulted in a permanent territorial gain for the Republic, it might have lent strength to Negrín's contention that the Republicans must continue to resist. It might also, therefore, have provided a common aim to bind together the different political strands of the Republican political fabric. But the Ebro campaign had failed, after four long, hard months of struggle. The Nationalist armies, once regrouped and refreshed would now undoubtedly attack both Catalonia and Valencia. Franco had said as much at the end of October to the head of the German intelligence services, Admiral Canaris, informing him at the same time that, in order to achieve their objectives, the Nationalists would need to take Hitler up on his promises of further supplies.[1]

Republican hopes of changes in international politics favourable to them had dwindled to nothing by the end of the summer. In the spring of 1938, it had looked as though Hitler's expansionist ambitions in Europe would provoke a war with France, Great Britain and Russia, and both sides began preparations for such an eventuality. However, in an eleventh hour attempt to avoid war by giving in to Hitler's territorial claims, an agreement was signed in Munich, on 29 September 1938, between the governments of France, Great Britain, Germany and Italy, whereby Czechoslovakia was virtually handed over to Hitler. The western democracies had, in effect, pulled the rug from under the feet of the Spanish Prime Minister. Those who, like Prieto, some of Largo Caballero's followers and the left-Republicans, favoured surrender or a negotiated end to hostilities were more than ever convinced that they could not hope for salvation through war in Europe and, therefore, that the war in Spain must end. President Azaña was of the same opinion. They could not know that, within a year of its signature, the Munich Pact would be like so much waste paper. They only knew that all the resources once possessed by the Republic were on the verge of total exhaustion.

For two years, all over Spain, terrified civilians had been fleeing as best they might with their goods and chattels hastily gathered into bundles to take with them. The same scenes of utter panic now began in Catalonia, except that, by the autumn of 1938, the only place left to go was across the border into France. Even Negrín began to ask himself when the killing and the running would stop. Continually accused by fellow socialists

93

and others of having fallen too far under the sway of the Communist Party, Negrín resolved to show that he was, first and foremost, a defender of democracy. The churches had been closed in the Republican zone since 10 August 1936; now, it became possible again to celebrate mass in private establishments (though not in the churches). The POUM members arrested in May 1937 were brought to trial in October 1938 and were given considerably fairer and more lenient treatment by the Republican courts than had been meted out to their unfortunate leader, Andreu Nin, by Stalin's police. The most significant gesture, however, was the departure, in November 1938, of the surviving International Brigaders, in accordance with an announcement made by Negrín to the League of Nations on 21 September 1938.[2] The Republic now had to rely almost exclusively on its own resources, for Soviet aid had decreased considerably as the USSR turned its political and military attention to preparation for a possible conflict with Germany.

The Nationalists, by contrast, could still rely on German assistance, which flowed in abundantly following an economic agreement signed between Hitler's and Franco's government in November 1938. As a result, the Nationalists were able to end 1938 with an all-out attack along the entire Catalan front. This was, in fact, the beginning of the end of the civil war and of the Second Spanish Republic.

Throughout December 1938, Nationalist planes subjected the inhabitants of the east coast to their fourth successive month of bombardment. As Italian and German pilots repeatedly targeted the ports, railways, power stations and factories of Catalonia, the civilian population was constantly obliged to run for the air-raid shelters and, later, to search for dead and survivors under tons of rubble. The Catalans, who, until 1938, had been relatively isolated from the active theatres of war, were now in the front line and began to suffer all the hardships and fears that their Andalusian, Basque, Galician, Asturian and *madrileño* compatriots had already been through. In addition to the loss of their homes, their belongings and their families, food and fuel were running short. The rain and cold of winter were an added misery. Bad weather retarded the Nationalist overland advance for several days, but by the third week of December, Franco had decided to wait no longer. Ignoring a plea from the papal nuncio to suspend the fighting over Christmas, Franco, the self-appointed 'saviour' of Christianity, launched 300,000 soldiers into attack on 23 December 1938. By the end of the year, they had advanced well into Catalonia, taking hundreds of prisoners as they occupied one village after another.

In spite of the fact that the war was clearly lost, in spite of the lack of armaments in even reasonable condition and in spite of the war-weariness of both troops and civilians, the Republican military command decided to launch a final, desperate attempt to delay the inevitable Nationalist occupation of Catalonia. Hundreds of kilometres away, in the Andalusian province of Córdoba, an attack was launched on 9 January 1939. In the first instance, as had happened at Brunete and at the Ebro, the element of surprise gave the Republicans the advantage, but they could not turn this into a victory. The fighting dragged on until the beginning of February but ultimately ended in defeat for the Republicans.

The aim of the Córdoba offensive had been to draw Nationalist attention away from the Catalonia, but it did not even succeed in doing that much. The Nationalist advance continued apace in the north-east corner of the peninsula, while thousands of frightened, desperate civilians and soldiers fled to cross the border into France. In the three weeks following the start of the Catalan offensive, Franco's armies had occupied more than twenty towns, advancing by an average of 8 to 10 kilometres each day. On 15 January, the Nationalists entered Tarragona and occupied the greater part of the province of which it was the capital. A week later, it was the turn of the coastal resort of Sitges, and by 24 January, they had reached and taken the textile mills and factories of the industrial towns surrounding Barcelona. A despatch from Franco's General Staff on 25 January stated that a total of 350,000 prisoners had been taken. On the following day, General Yagüe entered Barcelona at the head of Nationalist troops and the Littorio Division of the Italian army.

In Barcelona, as happened each time the Nationalists entered a new town or village, the occupying forces were greeted by ecstatic Nationalist supporters who now dared to profess their sympathies openly. Many carried large portraits of Franco or wore the blue shirt of FET y de las JONS, although in truth, many of those who now donned the party uniform did so not because they had always been card-holding Falange members but because this was the most easily recognizable sign of being a partisan of the winning side. Falangist banners and the red and yellow flag of Nationalist Spain were draped over balconies in salute to the 'liberators' of Barcelona. Crowds of people thronged the streets, giving the fascist salute (which had been adopted as the official mode of salute on 24 April 1937) as the victorious troops marched down the same boulevards that had witnessed the parade of the departing International Brigaders just two months earlier. In the wake of the troops came the trucks of the party's aid department, 'Social Assistance', from which girls in party uniform distributed bread. After the troops and the party members came the third pillar of the Francoist state, the Catholic church. Priests and nuns came out of hiding and rapidly re-established the practice of Catholicism openly and in whatever church buildings had not been burnt down or desecrated. Indeed, one of the first events after the occupation of Barcelona was the celebration of an open-air mass in the centre of the city, attended by a vast crowd of soldiers and civilians.

The Republican government had left Barcelona on 25 January 1939, accompanied by the respective Presidents of the Basque and Catalan regional governments, José Antonio Aguirre and LLuis Companys. Martial law had finally been declared in the Republican zone on 23 January and one man – General Miaja – had been given direct command of all the Republican armed forces. With hindsight we can say that it was not until within three months of the end of the war that the Republicans took these two vital military steps, taken by the

Nationalists within three months of its beginning. The course of the war and the situation in January 1939 were eloquent and terrible testimony of the wisdom of the Nationalist choice.

The Republican government established itself temporarily in the town of Figueras, 25 km from the French border. There, on 1 February 1939, the sixty-seven remaining Republican parliamentary representatives held what was to be their last session in Spain. By then, the government had ceased to speak of resistance and was solely concerned with securing an end to the war which would ensure the physical safety of the defeated. At the 1 February meeting, the Prime Minister, Juan Negrín, put forward a three-point proposal which stated the Republicans' conditions for an end to the war. These were that the Nationalists should guarantee Spanish independence from foreign intervention, that all Spaniards might take part in a plebiscite to determine what form of government should be adopted, and that there should be no reprisals. Negrín's plan was accepted, and a vote of confidence in his government was passed. The three-point peace proposal was subsequently given to French and British intermediaries for transmission to Franco.

If anyone in Republican territory had time to spare from preserving their own safety for considering the doings of the politicians, they may well have thought the Figueras parliamentary session at worst a waste of precious time or, at best, simply irrelevant. The action of the President of the Republic, Manuel Azaña, was far more expressive of the stark reality of the situation: on 5 February, in the company of regional Presidents Companys and Aguirre, he crossed the French frontier, leaving the mass of those who had fought to defend the Republic to their fate. Two days later, the Republican government crossed into France, followed by Prime Minister Negrín on 8 February. By 9 February 1939, the Nationalists had reached all the Pyrenean border posts in Catalonia. The Catalan campaign was over. Now, only the triangle encompassing Madrid, Valencia and Almería still resisted.

The fall of Catalonia was as much a psychological as a military victory for the Nationalists. News of the massive flight

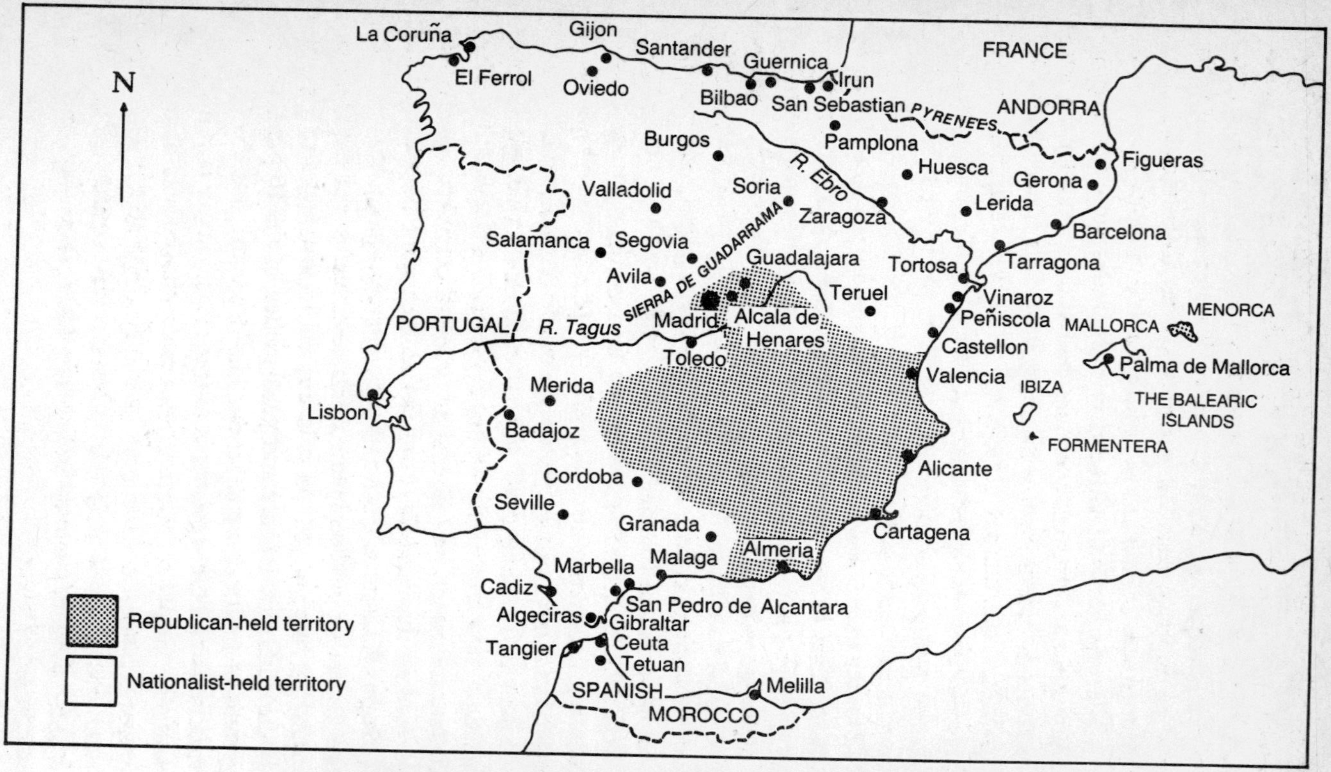

MAP 2 Republican and Nationalist Positions in February 1939

of refugees from what had been a stronghold of Republican resistance, together with reports of the appalling conditions they suffered in the makeshift camps hurriedly set up by the French government, had a powerful demoralizing effect on the civilians and troops in the territory still in Republican hands. The apparent invincibility of Franco's armies and the knowledge that both the Republican head of state and a large contingent of ministers and top civil servants had left the country further convinced Republicans that their cause was lost. Once Catalonia had fallen, the central Republican zone was surrounded on three sides by Nationalist territory and, on the fourth, by the sea. In such circumstances, what little was left of people's fighting spirit was under severe strain.

It was also an economic victory for Franco because the area around Madrid was now cut off from the — albeit minimal — supplies of food and munitions which had been coming from Catalonia. Moreover, the Republic's credit with foreign powers was at a low ebb. Even where an official policy of non-intervention did not impose an arms embargo, foreign governments were reluctant to advance money or munitions to a state whose own President and Prime Minister had fled and whose possibilities of overcoming a technically, physically and psychologically superior enemy were practically non-existent.

Finally, the occupation of Catalonia was a political victory because it left the Republic effectively 'decapitated'. The absence of the Prime Minister and the cabinet left the processes of central responsibility and decision-making in suspension. This was disastrous enough from a practical point of view, but the departure of President Azaña also had a deeper significance. As head of state, Azaña was the incarnation and symbol of the authority, legality and permanence of the Republic as a system of political organization. His departure left the formal structures and the legal status of that system intact but divested it of its capacity to exercise supreme authority and, therefore, jeopardized its permanence. With Azaña's post vacant, the state could be occupied by whoever was strong enough to impose their hegemony. In January 1939, there was only one contender: Franco.

It is scarcely surprising that the crumbling of the Republican state reopened the deep divisions between the various components of the Republican political camp. They had been camouflaged or contained since April 1938 by a precarious governmental unity and a desperate voluntarism but now came fully into the open and with increased vehemence. Broadly speaking, there were two groups: on the one hand, a small number of socialists and the communists; on the other, the non-communist army leaders, the anarchists, left-Republicans and the majority of the socialists. This division ultimately crystallized around two figures: Juan Negrín, head of the Republican government, and Colonel Segismundo Casado, chief of the Republican Army of the Centre. At the beginning of February, as Azaña and the regional presidents crossed the frontier into France, Casado had a secret meeting in Madrid with a Francoist agent. Two days earlier, Casado had discussed with socialist Julián Besteiro what they both considered the urgent and unquestionable necessity of trying to negotiate peace with Franco. It was this proposal that Casado put to Franco's emissary on 5 February 1939. His view was reinforced by Azaña's refusal to return to Spain and by the advice given by the Superintendent of Supplies, Francisco Méndez Aspe, to the effect that food should not be sent to Madrid, the implication being that it would be effort wasted.

The Communist Party, by contrast, maintained that resistance was still possible and remonstrated against what it saw as the defeatist attitude of their political rivals. Negrín had left Spain on 8 February but returned two days later, accompanied by a group of ministers and communist leaders. An official press release issued on 13 February stated that their position was of no surrender. This was understandable in the light of Franco's 'response' to the three-point peace plan Negrín had offered after the Figueras parliamentary session. On 11 February, the *generalísimo* had signed the Law of Political Responsibilities, which indicated that there would be no mercy for anyone considered to have held even the most minor political post under the Republic or to have 'obstructed' the Nationalist cause; and 'obstruction' would, of course, be defined by the

Nationalists. Moreover, this Draconian law was retroactive to October 1934, which greatly increased the numbers of people who might be caught up in its repressive drag-net. In these circumstances, the idea of peace negotiations was simply irrelevant.

Such, perhaps, was the reasoning behind Negrín's failure to respond to a British offer of mediation, made through the Republican Ambassador in London, Pablo Azcárate, on 16 February. It was certainly the gist of Negrín's position as he expressed it at a meeting with the leaders of the armed forces near Valencia on 26 February. The military men did not share Negrín's view that resistance was possible. Their scepticism seemed immediately to be confirmed by events: on 27 February, the French parliament voted that *de jure* recognition be conceded to Franco's Spain. Britain, too, decided to recognize Franco and his cabinet as the legitimate government of the Spanish state. On that same day, Manuel Azaña resigned as President of the Republic.

It appears that it was after the 26 February meeting that the anti-resistance lobby decided to try to oust Negrín. Their revolt began when it became known, at the beginning of March 1939, that the Prime Minister had made a series of changes and promotions in the military hierarchy which favoured communist officers. The non-communist military men were incensed by the promotion of communists Juan Modesto, Antonio Cordón, Enrique Lister, Manuel Tagueña, Antonio Galán and Etelvino Vega to the leadership of the divisions in the zones remaining under Republican control. The first protest was a confused episode at the naval base in Cartagena. There, a minor coup was effected against the newly appointed Antonio Galán, and although troops loyal to the government eventually got the situation under control, it was not before a group of Falangist sympathizers had taken advantage of the confusion to get a message to Franco asking for help. This duly arrived, in the form of a number of battleships. In view of the situation at the naval base, the chief of the Republican fleet decided not to take the fleet into Cartagena. Instead, he surrendered to France, whereupon he was instructed to put in at the Tunisian port of Bizerta. Since, by then, France had officially recognized Franco's government, the ships were incorporated into the Nationalist fleet, leaving the Republic without a navy.

While all this was taking place in Cartagena, Colonel Casado announced in Madrid that a National Defence Council had been created. It was headed by General Miaja and was composed of representatives of all the leftist Republican political organizations, with the exception of the Communist Party. Casado himself was also a member. In a manifesto broadcast by radio with the midnight war report on 5 March 1939, the Council announced that it had taken over the powers of government it considered had been illegally assumed, abused and, finally, abandoned by the Negrín cabinet. The Council pledged its determination that no one should desert nor shirk his or her responsibilities and proposed a negotiated end to hostilities.

What had taken place was, in effect, a *pronunciamiento* against Negrín, who left Spain definitively on 6 March 1939. More than that, however, the creation of the Defence Council represented the final disintegration of the political fabric of the Republic and brought to a head the tension which had been growing between the PSOE and the PCE since 1937. Madrid now became the scene of a civil war within the civil war, as the communists reacted against the Council's coup and the latter fought back. By 9 March, the communists had gained the upper hand in Madrid, after intense fighting in the city centre. It is possible that they could have won in the capital, but they were virtually marooned there, for the Defence Council controlled the rest of the centre-south zone, and as we noted earlier, this was itself surrounded on three sides by Nationalist territory and on the fourth by the sea. Consequently, there was little point for the PCE in defeating Casado's forces in Madrid. At most, the communists' show of strength placed them in a better position to negotiate with the Council a no-reprisals end to hostilities. By 13 March, the counter-coup was over.

The Defence Council immediately resumed its attempts to negotiate with Franco. The Nationalist terms for an end to hostilities, known as the *Generalísimo's Concessions*, amounted to what had been Franco's demand all along: unconditional surrender. Moreover, they seemed to leave ample scope for subsequent reprisals. Given the scale of repression already undertaken in newly conquered Republican territory and the existence of the Law of Political Responsibilities, there was every reason to suppose that the end of the war would be followed by massive and brutal retribution.

Franco's reply to the Defence Council came on 19 March 1939. As expected, it insisted that nothing short of total, unconditional surrender could be considered. The Council reduced its conditions to one: a period of twenty-five days to complete the evacuation of all who wished to leave the country. The Republicans must have known in advance that Franco would refuse, but they needed to play for time. While each side considered the other's proposals, Casado had set about creating central and provincial committees to take charge of the evacuation. He had also planned the withdrawal of the Army of the Centre from Madrid, to cover the retreat. All this was done in secrecy, and the application of the evacuation plan was delayed because some of the Defence Council's members apparently feared that its implementation would totally demoralize the civilian population and the army. This was a curious line of reasoning, to say the least, given that the armed forces and the civilian population from which it was drawn had suffered – and survived – nearly three years of war and that those same people now had absolutely no possibility of tasting the fruits of victory. The least to which they had a right was information which would enable them to decide whether or not to remain in Madrid. The Council evidently thought otherwise and not only did not inform the public of what it was doing but also postponed the execution of the evacuation plan until 26 March.

The Nationalist agents returned on 21 March, asking for two military negotiators to be nominated. The two agreed upon were a bizarre choice: one was suspected of Nationalist sympathies and the other was subsequently decorated by Franco for services rendered! Talks began on 23 March, at an airfield near Burgos. The Council's representatives asked for clarification of some of the *generalísimo*'s 'concessions' and stated that the Republicans would need almost a month to organize a surrender. The Nationalists, however, argued that capitulation must be immediate and total. The Defence Council spokesmen responded that this was impossible. In addition, they insisted that any agreement must be made in writing and that it must be made clear who would be considered eligible for the death penalty. Discussion had been resumed on 25 March when a message from Franco brought the talks to an abrupt end. The reason given was that the Republican air force had not been surrendered as demanded.

The following day, Franco indicated to the Defence Council that his armies were about to begin their final advance and that the Republican forces should show the white flag on all fronts if they wished to avoid artillery and aerial attacks. The Defence Council advised all units to surrender and itself prepared to withdraw to Valencia. The Republican army now virtually disintegrated, as its war-weary troops surrendered to the Nationalists or simply left their positions to go home. Many did so in the belief that, as they had had no political responsibilities before or during the conflict, they would be able to take up their lives again where they had left off in 1936. Franco, however, considered that all who had not been actively for him were, *ipso facto*, against him. In his view, all who had not defended the Nationalist cause were 'anti-Spain' and must now purge their guilt. Hundreds of thousands of prisoners were taken as the Nationalists completed their occupation of Republican territory, confirming Republican fears that, with Franco in command, peace might well be almost indistinguishable from war.

NOTES

1. Hitler's offer was made on 1 October 1938, through the German Ambassador in Nationalist Spain, Baron von Stohrer.

2. This was an attempt at *rapprochement* with France and Britain, in the belief that war with Hitler was imminent. Mussolini had withdrawn 10,000 Italian soldiers in October 1938, but German and Italian aid to Franco still gave the Nationalists quantitative and qualitative superiority over the Republicans.

8

The End of the War. The Aftermath

For the mass of the population, the evacuation was a shambles. The Defence Council had requested the respective Presidents of France and Mexico to allow the entry of Spanish refugees into their countries, but beyond this, it had failed to take adequate steps to organize the operation nationally or internationally. Contact had been made with Dr Negrín and the Superintendent of Supplies, Méndez Aspe, in Paris on 17 March, in an attempt to secure the services of a Republican-owned British company, the Mid-Atlantic Shipping Company, but the attempt failed. On 23 March, Besteiro and Casado met the French and British Consuls in Alicante. The former told them that the French government would probably exercise certain restrictions with regard to the entry of refugees, but he would need at least three days to verify this. The British diplomat, in response to the request for ships for the evacuation, replied that the British government would raise no objections, provided that General Franco agreed.

While the Defence Council tried belatedly to organize some means of escape, thousands of refugees congregated at the Mediterranean ports still held by the Republic. In Alicante, 3,500 were able to embark on a British ship, while another 1,500 or 2,000 escaped on four or five other ships. Whatever the exact number of those who managed to get away, it certainly was not 'all those who so desired', as the Defence Council's manifesto had promised. It was not even the 30,000 that one of Negrín's aides later claimed could have been evacuated had the Casado coup not prevented the execution of the government's plan. Of those who could not escape to the very relative security of exile, some committed suicide in sheer desperation and dread; thousands of others were rounded up and put into Nationalist concentration camps and prisons already overflowing with the victims of three years of persecution. In all, some two million people suffered imprisonment because their ideas were intolerable to General Franco and his partisans.[1]

The most important objective for the Nationalists was still, as it had been for three years, Madrid. What they had initially believed they would achieve by 25 July 1936 finally occurred on 27 March 1939. On that day, Colonel Casado ordered the chief of the Republican Army of the Centre to surrender his troops to the leader of the Nationalist forces on the Madrid front. Towards midday on 27 March, the Nationalist General Espinosa de los Monteros entered the capital. With 'their people' in command of Madrid, Nationalist sympathizers who had spent three years in hiding or, at least, in silence, emerged to receive their liberators. Crowds of people lined the streets, giving the fascist salute and cheering, as truck loads of Nationalist troops drove into the city. Nationalist and Falangist flags appeared everywhere. Priests and nuns put on their religious habits again without fear of reprisal. And the chant of 'Franco! Franco! Franco!' was shouted incessantly by his euphoric supporters.

On the same day, as the advance of the Nationalist troops reduced Republican territory to a small pocket on the east coast, Colonel Casado and seventy-four members of the Defence Council and its administrative staff managed to embark at Gandía, near Valencia, on a British ship, after lengthy and tense discussion with the ship's captain and the British Consul in Alicante. Casado found refuge in London and eventually returned to Spain in the 1960s. He was then tried by a court martial and, astonishingly, found not guilty. The man who had read the Council's manifesto into the radio microphone on 5 March, Julián Besteiro, was less fortunate. Having decided that it was his duty to stay behind, he was arrested and subsequently sentenced by a Francoist military tribunal to thirty years imprisonment. At his trial, the prosecutor was a man who had once been one of Besteiro's own students. His remarks exuded the intolerance of others' beliefs which had led to the war and which was the hallmark of Francoism. 'Besteiro's case,' he said, 'is typical of the Spanish revolution ... I have to say that Julián Besteiro's actions have had nothing but seriously erroneous results for the country and for himself, victim as he is of his own mistakes ... [He] is wicked, terribly wicked, in Spanish politics. He is pernicious to the Fatherland.'[2] Besteiro died in prison of blood poisoning in 1940.

Between 27 and 31 March, the provinces of Cuenca, Guadalajara, Ciudad Real, Jaén, Albacete, Almería, Murcia, Alicante and Valencia were incorporated into the Francoist 'New State'. On 1 April 1939, in Burgos, Franco signed the final was bulletin, which read: 'On this day, with the red army captive and disarmed, the Nationalist army has achieved its final military objectives. The war has ended.'[3]

It was no mere syntactical nicety that the last Nationalist war bulletin referred to 'final *military* objectives', for the post-war ordeal suffered by the defeated was every bit as terrible and even longer lasting than the three years of the armed conflict. For the Francoists, the fight would go on for as long as there remained in Spain any vestige of beliefs different to their own. It is difficult to know with certainty how many people were executed after the war. Some foreign observers estimated that at least 10,000 people had been shot up to the end of August 1939;[4] official statistics admitted to 'only' 15,000 in the two-year period 1939–40.[5] A Spanish historian who fought with the Carlists regards 28,000 as the 'probable' figure for the decade 1941–1950.[6] By any standards, the scale of such reprisals was sickening.

In addition to those killed or imprisoned by the Francoist authorities, thousands more lived hunted existences, in constant fear of detection; many actually went into hiding in their own homes, not to emerge from attics, cellars and other, more bizarre hidey-holes until years later.[7] Yet more left their country for exile all over the world, particularly in Latin America, Mexico, France and Belgium. Some — a minority — prospered in their countries of forced adoption. Some of those countries, too, benefitted from the presence of the refugees. Economic development in Mexico, for example, owed much to the skills and labours of exiled Spanish workers, professionals and intellectuals. Most of the outcasts, however, were obliged to eke out their sad existences doing whatever work they could find. More often than not, this meant accepting employment, wages and conditions far removed from what they had known before the war. In addition to the bitterness of defeat, the anguish of leaving their country and the material misery of exile, there was, thus, the additional trauma of being forcibly transformed from army officer, doctor, teacher, journalist, barber, printer, baker or whatever, into Displaced Person.

Yet the Republicans' spirit was not broken, nor their ideals crushed. Even in prison, groups of socialists and communists kept alive their political faith and even managed to produce hand-written clandestine editions of their pre-war newspapers. When war finally broke out in Europe, in September 1939, many of those who had managed to leave Spain continued to fight fascism as members of resistance movements. Some, like the former Prime Minister, Largo Caballero, were caught and sent to concentration camps in Germany and Austria or put to work in Nazi labour camps in other parts of occupied Europe. Others, like the former President of Catalonia, LLuis Companys, were arrested and turned over to the Francoist police, in whose hands they were often brutally tortured before being executed. There were concentration camps inside Spain, too, for those who, having lost the war, could not or did not choose to abandon their country. Large numbers of prisoners were used as a cheap labour force for the reconstruction of roads, bridges and railways and for the excavation and building of a huge, underground basilica in the Guadarrama mountains, which was to be a memorial to the Nationalist dead and Franco's own tomb. To make defeated Republicans build a pharaonic monument to their persecutors was a gesture of particularly vindictive cruelty.

To the hardships occasioned by the war were soon to be added new ones of shortages of food, clothing and housing, lack of medicines and dwindling supplies of fuel of all kinds. Between 1936 and 1939, some 2,500 people had died of malnutrition. In the first post-war decade, known by the Spaniards themselves as 'the hungry years', many more died of the same 'disease' and of destitution, illness and injury. It does not seem exaggerated to say that some people probably died of sheer sadness. There are no statistics which specifically reflect their pain, but the average annual number of known suicides rose from 1,339 for the period 1931−5, to 1,719 for 1939−42, and 1,549 for the decade between 1941 and 1950.[8] Franco and his partisans 'explained' the problems as the result of the 'chaos' brought by the Republic, or as the work of 'anti-Spain' subversives, but few can have been deceived. The adviser on international economic affairs to the US State Department, Herbert Feis, made a shrewd assessment of Spain's situation in May 1939;

> The production of food, coal, cloth, shoes and fertilizers, all remained very low. Whatever propaganda can do, it cannot plow or fertilize the soil. Coal seams cannot be broken down by police standing in the entrance to the mines; broken locomotives and trucks cannot be made to run by the dirty grease of oratory; cotton mills cannot spin threats.[9]

These were difficulties which did not distinguish so much between victors and vanquished as between rich and poor, between those who could buy scarce goods on the black market and those who could not. Many of those who, in 1939 and 1940, stood in the endless queues for rationed bread, sugar, potatoes, milk or coal must have asked themselves if it was for this that they had endured the war.

Some of those who had conspired actively to bring the war about may have asked themselves the same question as they stood on the platform adjoining the elaborate dais from which Franco took the salute at the victory parade held in Madrid on

19 May 1939. Franco watched with evident satisfaction as the tanks trundled down Madrid's central boulevard, followed by row upon row of soldiers, Civil Guards, Falangists, sailors, Moroccan guards and Legionnaires. The partisans of the Carlist and Alfonsist dynasties, the national syndicalists of the Falange and the authoritarian Catholics of the various conservative parties, now all incorporated into the 'single party' of which Franco was the head, may well have wondered whether the *generalísimo* had not stolen a march on them. The Republic had been destroyed, as they had wished; but they had not bargained on its being replaced by a dictatorship in which all power was vested in one man. Such, however, was the reality which had emerged from the war. As Spaniards who had served in and behind both sets of battle lines were to discover, it was a reality with which they would have to live for the best part of the next forty years.

How it was that the Franco regime lasted so long lies beyond the scope of the present volume, but what we can say here is that its longevity was partly due to the way in which it razed the Republic to the ground between 1936 and 1939. Ultimately, Francoism's brute force proved incapable of eradicating the ideas and aspirations which had informed the Second Spanish Republic, but the fact that it had physically and morally crushed the trades unions and parties of the left and reformist centre meant that it took decades for them to regroup. Indeed, it was not until after Franco's death, in 1975, and the lifting of the ban on political parties and trades unions, that they were able to recoup anything like their former strength. Some of them, such as Republican Left or the anarchist CNT, never did recover from the blows inflicted by the war.

Yet, as we have seen, superior Nationalist might (in which must be included German, Italian and other foreign aid) was not solely responsible for the collapse of the Republic. In a well-established democracy, political diversity and dissent not only strengthen the system, they are of its very essence. However, for reasons which had to do with the country's retarded socio-economic infrastructure, democracy was not firmly established in Spain in 1936. Consequently, the Republic's ca-

111

pacity to take internal conflict in its stride was very limited. Articulating parliamentary democracy in Spain between 1931 and 1936 was like attempting to organize a coherent game of football with each team trying to impose its own set of rules, some players squabbling with others on their own side, and no one taking any notice of the referee. Without consensus, at least on the minimal objective of implementing democratic rule, confrontation was inevitable; although this is not at all to say that the lack of consensus was also inevitable.

When confrontation had reached its maximum expression — war — both sides were faced with the necessity of binding diverse political, military and paramilitary groups into a united, efficiently coordinated force. Rebels and loyalists responded to this problem in radically different ways. Whereas the Nationalists immediately took steps to paralyse normal, civilian life, subjugating it to military authority, the Republicans endeavoured to keep separate the respective forms and functions of civil and military spheres until the final months of the war. By 1 October 1936, Francoist Spain had a single, all-powerful military and political leader. In the Republican zone, by contrast, regional and central governmental structures were still in existence when the war ended, and it was not until January 1939 that one, single military officer took direct command of all the Republican armed forces. Nationalists and Republicans also dealt differently with the problems posed by internal political conflicts. Certainly, there was a greater degree of consensus among the Nationalist groups about the need for a military victory in order to liquidate the Republic and the reformist, pluralist values it enshrined; but there was no unanimity about what kind of regime should be constructed after that victory had been achieved. In April 1937, Franco put a decisive stop to all speculation and jockeying for positions, with the Decree of Unification. The Republicans by contrast were not only more deeply divided in political terms, but no single group or individual had the monopoly of physical force that Franco possessed. This, together with the Republicans' commitment to the maintenance of democratic forms, made it more difficult for one group to impose its will on the others.

112

The initial reluctance or inability of socialists, communists and left-Republicans to impose on the anarchists and POUMists the view that the war must take precedence over social revolution effectively meant that respect for democratic rights and liberties was putting the survival of democracy at risk! On the other hand, by May 1937, once force had been used to enable one set of priorities to prevail over the other, that respect had been compromised. Thereafter, Republican democracy was eroded by the resurgent power of the state, whose coercive capacity was magnified precisely because of the exceptional (i.e. wartime) situation in which it had been reconstituted. The question of how far it is legitimate for democratic governments to impose decisions not seconded by significant numbers of the populace, or to disregard the norms of democratic practice in the national interest, is clearly not limited to what happened in Spain during the civil war; nor, indeed, to wartime. The failure of the Second Republic to resolve what, in the circumstances, was a tragic dilemma made a significant contribution to the outcome of the war. However, it is difficult to accept that the method adopted by the Nationalists − suppression of all dissent − was preferable.

Another question of universal relevance raised by the Spanish Civil War is that of the involvement of foreign powers in national conflicts. Taken with all the internal political factors, inhibition on the part of the western democracies, together with the active participation of Germany and Italy, undoubtedly swung the balance decisively in favour of Franco. But there was no guarantee that, were France, Britain or the United States to have assisted the Republic, their intervention would not have provoked the outbreak of war with Germany before the democratic powers were materially ready to resist. We now know that Hitler was determined to go to war; but this was not so clear-cut to the politicians of the time, and it could be argued that the policy of appeasement did at least buy three years of preparation time, even if it was secured by sacrificing democracy in Spain. However, we must take into account that the western governments were bound to do what they considered consistent with their own political interests. In this respect, it is

113

less surprising that a Conservative British government should be extremely wary of assisting Spanish leftists than it is that a French Popular Front government should be unwilling to do so. In the final analysis, the German threat to France was more powerful than feelings of ideological solidarity with Spain.

It might have been expected that, in the ultimate adversity of defeat, the defenders of the Second Spanish Republic would bury their differences in the interests of survival, if not of trying to unseat Franco by diplomatic means, particularly following the defeat of fascism in 1945. In fact, no such thing happened. Successive Republican governments in exile debated interminably what strategy to employ, and the different parties wrangled amongst themselves about who bore what portion of blame for the defeat. In time, new divisions emerged within the parties, with the views of an aging exiled leadership seen to be increasingly inappropriate to what was happening inside Spain, as this was experienced by new generations of clandestine activists. For despite the horrors of the war and the subsequent massive mobilization of all kinds of repressive resources, from censorship to firing squads, the spirit of democracy was still alive in Spain. As Spain developed socially and economically into a modern, industrialized nation in the 1960s and 1970s, the restoration of democratic freedoms became the aspiration of a growing number of Spaniards of all social classes and of all but the most extreme rightist political persuasions.

When the death of General Franco in November 1975 opened the way to the fulfillment of that aspiration, there was present in Spain a powerful sense of having emerged from a long period of captivity. The new king, Don Juan Carlos I, immediately made it clear that the healing of the divisions of the past would be one of his deepest concerns. At his proclamation in Madrid on 22 November 1975, he announced that he intended to be king of *all* Spaniards, by which he meant that he wanted to be both the symbol and the instrument of a necessary reconciliation deliberately never undertaken by Franco.

Democracy is more firmly established in Spain today, both as a political system and as a cultural model, than it was at any time during the Second Republic. As a result of the rapid process of social and economic modernization undertaken in the 1960s, today's democratic institutions, unlike those of the 1930s, have sufficient strength to carry out their functions without provoking major conflict. In addition, there is a desire and a will on the part of new generations of Spaniards to experience life not as confrontation, but as consensus. The measure of how far Spain has travelled away from the intolerance and fear which led to the civil war is given by the realization that the possibility of its being repeated now seems as remote as a repetition of the English or American Civil Wars.

NOTES

1. P. Preston, *The Spanish Civil War, 1936–39*, London, Weidenfeld & Nicolson, 1990, p. 166.
2. M. Rubio Cabeza, *Diccionario de la guerra civil*, 2 vols, Barcelona, Planeta, 1987, vol. 1, p. 122.
3. Quoted in L. Suarez Fernández, *Francisco Franco y su tiempo*, 8 vols, Madrid, Fundación Nacional Francisco Franco, 1984, vol. 2 p. 345, n. 35.
4. Preston, op. cit., p. 167.
5. R. Salas Larrazabal, quoting Instituto Nacional de Estadística, 'Movimiento natural de la población de España', in J.M. Armero et al. *Historia del franquismo*, 2 vols, Madrid, Historia 16, 1985 vol. 1, p. 26.
6. Ibid., p. 29.
7. See, for example, R. Fraser, *In Hiding. The Life of Manuel Cortés*, London, Allen Lane, 1972.
8. Salas, op. cit., p. 22. It seems likely that this is an underestimation of the real figure.
9. H. Feis, *The Spanish Story*, 1948; New York, Norton, 1966, p. 7.

Further Reading

A great many books have been written about the Spanish Civil War. Indeed, it is said that it has generated more volumes than the First and Second World Wars together! The following bibliography is not, of course, exhaustive, and it covers only volumes available in English. It is intended to help readers to focus in greater detail on some of the issues raised in the foregoing pages and to direct them towards different views of the war, its causes and repercussions. Multilingual readers will find in most of the books cited numerous further references to works written in languages other than English, especially to the very large bibliography which exists in Spanish. Unless otherwise stated, the place of publication is London. Volumes available in paperback are marked with an asterisk.

There are a number of interpretive 'summaries' of the period 1931–1939, of which the best is probably Raymond Carr, *The Civil War in Spain*, Weidenfeld & Nicolson, 1986. This is closely followed in excellence by two illustrated volumes, both of which convey the atmosphere of the period very well, in addition to providing lucid analysis of the issues: Paul Preston, *The Spanish Civil War, 1936–39**, Weidenfeld & Nicolson, 1990; and Gabriel Jackson, *A Concise History of the Spanish Civil War**, Thames and Hudson, 1974.

Many longer studies of the war and its antecedents also exist. If one were obliged to select only one account of the background to the war, Gerald Brenan's *The Spanish Labyrinth**, Cambridge University Press, 1943, would take pride of place. Although written nearly half a century ago, its insights have not dated and it still remains the most illuminating study of social, economic and political conditions in pre-

Civil War Spain. If one's 'minimum quota' were expanded to two volumes, then the second would undoubtedly be Raymond Carr, *Modern Spain, 1875–1980**, Oxford University Press, 1980, or his much longer *Spain, 1808–1975**, Oxford University Press, 1982. Both of these deal extensively with the nineteenth century and the post-Civil War period, thereby enabling the reader to identify and understand the place of the Second Republic and the war in the continuing stream of history. Gabriel Jackson's *The Spanish Republic and the Civil War**, Princeton, NJ, Princeton University Press, 1965, is a more detailed predecessor of the volume cited above. Hugh Thomas, *The Spanish Civil War**, Harmondsworth, Penguin, 1986, is packed with detailed information, but its density and length may make it a daunting prospect for relative newcomers to the subject. (In the edition published in Spanish by Editorial Urbión, Madrid, 1980, the text is accompanied by the best selection of graphic material available anywhere to date.) Two collective volumes should also be mentioned among those which provide a wide-ranging over-view of the Civil War and the period leading up to it: Martin Blinkhorn, ed., *Spain in Conflict*, Sage, 1986, and Paul Preston, ed., *Revolution and War in Spain, 1931–1939*, Methuen, 1984.

The political origins of the war are more specifically analysed by Paul Preston in his compelling study of both the right and the left of the contemporary political spectrum, *The Coming of the Spanish Civil War**, Methuen, 1983. A conservative interpretation of the political issues at stake between 1931 and 1939 is given in Richard A.H. Robinson, *The Origins of Franco's Spain*, Newton Abbot, David & Charles, 1970. The creation and significance of the Popular Front in France and Spain is examined in Michael Alexander and Helen Graham, eds, *The French and Spanish Popular Fronts. Comparative Perspectives*, Cambridge University Press, 1989, while the essays in Helen Graham and Paul Preston, eds, *The Popular Front in Europe*, Macmillan, 1987, provide a wider-ranging study of left-wing politics in the 1930s, covering Germany, France, Austria, Spain, Italy and the USSR. Helen Graham's monographic volume, *Socialism and War: The Spanish Socialist Party in Power and Crisis, 1936–1939* Cambridge University Press, 1991, is essential to an understanding of the role of the Spanish Socialist Party during the war. The contribution of the right to the collapse of the Republic and to the subsequent war is analysed in R.M. Blinkhorn's *Carlism and Crisis in Spain, 1931–1939*, Cambridge University Press, 1975; in Sheelagh Ellwood's *Spanish Fascism in the Franco Era*, Macmillan, 1987; and in Stanley G. Payne's,

Falange: A History of Spanish Fascism*, Stanford, CA, Stanford University Press, 1971.

Not surprisingly, given the passion and interest that the war generated world-wide, there are many contemporary accounts and memoirs by people who witnessed or were involved in the conflict in one way or another. Unfortunately, English translations of Spanish accounts of the war are not plentiful. Those which do exist, however, are well worth reading, although it must be borne in mind that, by their very nature, they are scarcely impartial. For example, the versions given by Julio Alvarez del Vayo (one-time Foreign Minister in the Republican government) in *Freedom's Battle*, Heinemann, 1940; Constancia de la Mora in *In Place of Splendour*, Michael Joseph, 1940; and Dolores Ibarruri in *They Shall Not Pass**, Lawrence and Wishart, 1967, are favourable to the Spanish Communist Party. Book 3 (*The Clash*) of Arturo Barea's three-part autobiography *The Forging of a Rebel**, Davis-Poynter, 1972, tells of the author's experiences as a journalist in Spain's beleagured capital after the outbreak of war (Books 1, *The Forge*, and 2, *The Track*, which cover the monarchy, the war in Morocco, the Primo de Rivera dictatorship and the Republic, are also well worth reading). Antonio Bahamonde's *Memoirs of a Spanish Nationalist*, United Editorial, 1939, as its title implies, gives the view of a Francoist partisan. Colonel Segismundo Casado's *The Last Days of Madrid, The End of the Second Spanish Republic*, Peter Davies, 1939, was clearly written by way of justification for his coup in March 1939; the Spanish edition, published a number of years later, contains some interesting discrepancies with the original English edition.

The US ambassador to Spain between 1933 and 1939, Claude Bowers, subsequently recorded his memory of the period in *My Mission to Spain*, Gollancz, 1954. In another account based on personal experience, the United Press correspondent in Spain during the war, Burnett Bolloten, condemns the communist' destruction of the anarchist- and socialist-led popular revolution in his book, *The Spanish Revolution, The Left and the Struggle for Power during the Civil War*, Chapel Hill, University of North Carolina Press, 1979 (1961 and 1968 editions entitled *The Grand Camouflage*). To English-speakers, the best known eye-witness account is probably George Orwell's story of his experiences as an International Brigader in the Spring of 1937, *Homage to Catalonia**, Harmondsworth, Penguin, 1982 (first published 1938. This edition also includes an essay, 'Looking Back on the Spanish War', first published in 1953). Of the dozens of other volumes produced by or about the International Brigaders, three in particular are written with a good literary style and do not romanticize their subject: Bill Alexander, *British Volunteers for Liberty*, Lawrence and Wishart, 1982; Jason Gurney, *Crusade in Spain*, Faber, 1974; and Cecil Eby, *Between the Bullet and the Lie*, New York, Holt, Rinehart, Winston, 1969. There are fewer accounts by foreign volunteers in the Nationalist armies, but Peter Kemp's *Mine Were of Trouble*, Cassell, 1957, gives the view of a British member of Franco's forces.

Besides the attention given in some of the volumes mentioned above to the international dimensions of the Spanish war, foreign intervention — or the lack of it — is examined in a number of monographic studies. On the Nationalist side, John F. Coverdale, *Italian Intervention in the Spanish Civil War*, Princeton, NJ, Princeton University Press, 1975, gives a fascinating account of Italian military and diplomatic support for Franco, while *Documents on German Foreign Policy*, Series D, Volume III, HMSO, 1951, is a collection of official communications between the German Foreign Ministry and German diplomats in various countries (especially Italy and Spain) between July 1936 and July 1939. The most infamous episode of German intervention is the subject of Herbert Southworth's exhaustive *Guernica! Guernica! A Study of Journalism, Diplomacy, Propaganda and History* Berkeley, Los Angeles and London, University of California Press, 1977. On the Republican side, David Cattell's *Soviet Diplomacy and the Spanish Civil War*, Berkeley, Los Angeles and London, University of California Press, 1957, looks at the part played by the USSR in the conflict. Ivan Maisky's *Spanish Notebooks*, Hutchinson, 1966, examines (and condemns) the workings of the Non-Intervention Committee. David Wingeate-Pike, *Conjecture, Propaganda and Deceit and the Spanish Civil War**, Stanford, CA, California Institute of International Studies, 1968, looks at how the French press presented the war. The British stance is detailed in Jill Edwards, *The British Government and the Spanish Civil War 1936–1939*, Macmillan, 1979.

Some good work has been produced in Spanish on the social, economic and cultural aspects of the war, but few studies are available in English. Edward Malefakis, *Agrarian Reform and Peasant Revolution in Spain*, New Haven, Yale University Press, 1970, looks at the Republic's ill-fated attempt to modernize the Spanish countryside. Gaston Leval, *Collectives in the Spanish Revolution**, Freedom Press, 1975, gives an anarchist's view of the collectivization experience. Chapters 7 and 8 of Frances Lannon's book, *Privilege, Persecution and Prophecy. The Catholic Church in Spain, 1875–1975*, Oxford University Press, 1987, analyse the social, political and economic role of the Catholic Church during the Second Republic and the Civil War. Adrian Shubert traces the antecedents to the 'October Revolution' in Asturias in his book, *The Road to Revolution in Spain, The Coal Miners of Asturias, 1860–1934*, Urbana and Chicago, University of Illinois Press, 1987.

Recent work done in Spain on wartime and post-war repression is unfortunately not available in English. However, there are a number of books in English which convey the atmosphere of Franco's Spain during the first, very harsh, years of the regime. Gerald Brenan displays characteristic sensitivity and acumen in his description of a journey through the south and west of Spain shortly after the end of the war: *The Face of Spain* Turnstile Press, 1950, is difficult to get hold of but worth searching for. The first two British ambassadors to Madrid both wrote memoirs which bring out the oppressive mood prevalent in the country. Maurice Peterson, *Both Sides of the Curtain*, Constable, 1950, includes a chapter on the author's brief posting to Madrid in 1939. He was replaced in the autumn of that year by Sir Samuel Hoare, whose *Ambassador on Special Mission*, Collins, 1946, is an intriguing account of his efforts to ensure Spanish neutrality during the Second World War. Hoare's book is best read in conjunction with the recollections of the second half of the same period given by the US ambassador, Carlton J. Hayes, in his *Wartime Mission in Spain, 1942–1945*, New York, Macmillan, 1945. The most illuminating first-hand account of the first years of the Franco regime is Herbert Feis, *The Spanish Story**, New York, Norton, 1966 (first published in 1948), whose combination of chronicle, analysis and narrative description provides some brilliant insights into the workings of the system which had emerged from the Civil War. Finally, the part played by the armed forces and the Falange in creating and sustaining that system is the subject of Paul Preston's excellent interpretive study, *The Politics of Revenge*, Unwin Hyman, 1990.

Index

'accidentalism', 14
Acción Española, 14
Acción Nacional, 14, 16
Acción Popular, 14, 18
africanistas, see Army of Africa
Aguirre, José Antonio, 56, 96, 97
Alava, 31, 80
Albacete, 108
Alcalá de Henares, 40
Alcalá-Zamora, Niceto, 14, 21, 25, 26
alcazar of Toledo, *see* Toledo
Alfambra, River, 85
Alfonso XIII, 9, 10, 11
Alicante, 15, 45, 106, 108
Almería, 108
anarchism, 19,75; *see also* CNT, FAI
Andalusia, 6, 13, 15, 44, 45
Annual (Morocco), 9
Aragón, 6, 19, 32, 45, 81, 83, 85, 86
Army, 13; of Africa, 9, 28, 31, 33, 43, 49, 50, 79, 87, 111; intervention in politics, 8,

10, 17, 23; Popular, 61–2, 79, 86
Assault Guards, 25, 37, 77
Asturias, 32, 45, 52, 81; 1934 revolution, 19–20
Attlee, Clement, 66
Austria, 20, 86
Avila, 40
Azaña Díaz, Manuel, 21, 22, 23, 25, 37, 57, 77, 93, 97, 98, 101
Aznar, Admiral Juan Bautista, 10

Badajoz, 44
Baldwin, Stanley, 66
Balearic Islands, 24, 45, 52
Barcelona, 25, 26, 34–6, 75, 76–7, 87, 95–6
Basque Country, 56
Basque Nationalist Party, *see* PNV
Belchite, 82
Belgium, 47, 109
Berenguer, General Dámaso, 10
Besteiro, Julián, 100, 106,

107-8
Bilbao, 52, 66, 68-9, 80
'Black Biennium', 19
Borbón Parma, Javier de, 24
Britain, 46, 47, 59, 66, 82, 86, 93, 101, 106-7, 113, 114
Brunete, 78-9
Burgos, 31, 39, 55

Cabanellas, General Miguel, 25, 32, 42, 54
Cádiz, 33
Calvo Sotelo, José, 25
Canaris, Admiral, 47, 93
Canary Islands, 24
Cantalupo, Ambassador, 65
Carlism, 12, 24, 31, 38-9, 69, 70-1, 73-4, 111
Cartagena, 29, 101
Casado, Colonel Segismundo, 100, 102, 103, 106, 107
Casares Quiroga, Santiago, 26, 38
Castelló, General, 48
Castellón de la Plana, 90-1
Castile, 6, 13, 31, 32
Catalonia, 6, 19, 41, 45, 86, 87, 91, 93, 94-9; government, 41, 76, 77
Catholic Church, 6, 13, 15, 18, 35, 51-2, 96
'Catholic Monarchs', 6
CEDA, 18, 19, 69, 70-1
Ceuta, 28, 29
Chapaprieta, Joaquin, 21
Christianity, 5-6, 38
Ciudad Real, 108
Civil Guard, 19, 32, 35, 37, 40, 71, 111
CNT, 17, 35, 38, 59, 76, 77, 111

Comintern, 21, 22
Committee for National Defence, 42, 43
Committee for the Defence of Madrid, 59-60, 77
Committee of Anti-Fascist Militias, 36, 76
communists, see PCE
Companys, LLuis, 76, 77, 96, 97, 109
Comunión Tradicionalista, see Carlism
Confederación Española de Derechas Autónomas, see CEDA
Confederación Nacional del Trabajo, see CNT
Córdoba, 45, 95
Cuenca, 108
Czechoslovakia, 47, 93

Dávila, General Fidel, 68
Derecha Regional Valenciana, 16
Dollfuss, Chancellor, 20

Ebro, battle, 91-3; River 82
Eden, Anthony, 59
elections, general (1933) 17, (1936) 22; local (1931) 11
El Ferrol, 32
El Salvador, 58
Escofet, Federico, 35
Espinosa de los Monteros, General, 107
Euzkadi, see Basque Country
Extremadura, 13, 43, 44

FAI, 35, 76; see also anarchism, CNT
Falange Española, 18
Falange Española de las JONS,

18, 19, 24, 32, 33, 39, 61, 69, 70–1, 73–4
Falange Española Tradicionalista y de las JONS, *see* FET y de las JONS
Falangists, *see* Falange Española de las JONS
Fanjul, General Joaquin, 25, 37
Faupel, Ambassador von, 65, 74
FE, *see* Falange Española
FE de las JONS, *see* Falange Española de las JONS
Federación Anarquista Ibérica, *see* FAI
Ferdinand and Isabella, *see* 'Catholic Monarchs'
Fernández Buriel, General, 34
Fernández Cuesta, Raimundo, 83
FET y de las JONS, 74, 83, 85, 90, 96, 101, 111
Figueras, 97
Formentera, *see* Balearic Islands
France, 46, 82, 86, 87, 91, 93, 101, 106, 109, 113, 114
Franco Bahamonde, General Francisco, 19, 23, 24, 25, 26, 29–31, 33, 43, 44, 50, 54, 55, 59, 64, 68, 69, 71, 72, 73, 74, 75, 78, 82, 83, 84, 85, 89, 90, 91, 92, 95, 99, 100, 103, 104, 108, 109, 110, 111, 112, 113, 114
Franco Bahamonde, Nicolás, 54, 71

Galarza, Angel, 77
Galicia, 32, 46
Gandía, 107
García de la Herán, General, 37
García Escámez, Colonel, 40

Gazapo, Lieutenant Colonel, 28
Generalísimo, see Franco Bahamonde, General Francisco
Generalitat, see Catalonia, government
Germany, 20, 33, 46, 47, 57, 58, 63–4, 67–8, 84, 86, 91, 93, 94, 104, 113, 114
Gijón, 45, 81
Gil Robles, José María, 18, 20, 21, 23
Giral, José, 38, 48
Goded, General Manuel, 24, 25, 34, 36
González Carrasco, General, 34
Granada, 5
Guadalajara, 39, 40, 64–5, 108
Guadarrama, mountains, 40, 44, 52, 109; village, 41
Guatemala, 58
Guernica, 67–8
Guipúzcoa, 32, 80; *see also* Basque Country

Hedilla, Manuel, 73, 74
Hidalgo, Diego, 19
Hitler, Adolf, *see* Germany
Holland, 47
Huesca, 32, 45

Ibarruri, Dolores, 60
Ibiza, *see* Balearic Islands
International Brigades, 62–3, 64, 65, 94
Irún, 32, 49, 52
Italy, 33, 46, 47, 57, 58, 63, 64–5, 79, 86, 91, 93, 94, 96, 105, 113

Jaén, 108

Jarama Valley, 64
JONS, 18
Juan Carlos I, King, 114
Juntas de Ofensiva Nacional
    Sindicalista, *see* JONS
Juventudes Socialistas, 21, 33

Kindelán, General Alfredo, 53,
    54

Labour Charter, 85–6
Largo Caballero, Francisco, 14,
    22, 38, 48, 56, 59, 61, 77,
    93, 109
League of Nations, 82, 89, 94
León, 31
Lérida, 86, 87
Lerroux, Alejandro, 21
Luca de Tena, Ignacio, 31

Madrid, 15, 23, 24, 26, 37–8,
    41, 43, 44, 45, 49, 57,
    59–60, 63, 64–5, 78, 83,
    84, 87, 99, 100, 102, 103,
    107, 110
Málaga, 63
Mallorca, *see* Balearic Islands
Manises, 91
Martínez Barrio, Diego, 38
Maura, Miguel, 15
Melilla, 28, 29
Méndez Aspe, 100, 106
Menorca, *see* Balearic Islands
Mérida, 43
Mexico, 58, 109
Miaja, General, 59, 78, 96, 102
Mola, General Emilio, 24, 26,
    31, 38, 53, 65, 68
monarchism, Alfonsist, 14, 69,
    111
Morocco, 26, 28; Civil War in,

27, 29; Spanish war in,
    8–9, 10
Moslem occupation, 5–6
Munich Pact, 93
Murcia, 45, 108
Mussolini, Benito, *see* Italy

National Defence Committee,
    52, 53–4, 55
National Defence Council, 102,
    103, 104, 106, 107
Navarre, 24, 31, 38, 80
Negrín, Juan, 73, 84, 87, 89–90,
    91, 92, 93, 97, 100, 101,
    102, 106
Nín, Andreu, 78
Northern Defence Committee,
    69, 80

Ortiz de Zárate, Colonel, 39, 40
Orwell, George, 77
Oviedo, 45, 81
Ovsenko, Vladimir Antonov, 47

Pamplona, 24, 31
Partido Comunista de España,
    see PCE
Partido Obrero de Unificación
    Marxista, *see* POUM
Partido Socialista Obrero
    Español, *see* PSOE
Partit Socialist Unificat de
    Catalunya, *see* PSUC
PCE, 17, 21, 22, 60, 62, 75, 76,
    84, 87, 94, 100, 101, 102
Peñiscola, 89
Picasso, Pablo Ruiz, 68
Pla i Deniel, Bishop, 51
PNV, 56, 80, 81
Poland, 47
Popular Front, committees, 21;

in France, 114; in Spain, 21, 22, 48

Portela Valladares, Manuel, 21, 23

Portugal, 47, 58

POUM, 21, 76, 77–8, 94

Pozas, General, 59

Prieto, Indalecio, 14, 21, 77, 84, 86, 87, 93

Primo de Rivera, José Antonio, 18, 20, 23, 24, 73

Primo de Rivera y Orbaneja, General Miguel, 9, 10, 71

PSOE, 11, 17, 21, 102

PSUC, 76

Queipo de LLano, General Gonzalo, 25, 33, 45, 63

Radical Party, 21

Renovación Española, 18, 23, 70–1

Republican government, *see* Second Spanish Republic

Republican Left Party, 21, 111

Requeté, 31, 33

Ríos, Fernando de los, 14

Rojo, Colonel, 65, 78

Rosenberg, Marcel, 47

Ruiz Picasso, Pablo, *see* Picasso

Russian aid, *see* Soviet Union

Sagunto, 91

Salamanca, 31, 55

Sanjurjo, General José, 23, 53

San Sebastian, 45, 46, 52; pact of, 10

Santander, 32, 78, 79–81

Santoña, 80

Saravia, Colonel, 48

Segovia, 31

Serrano Suñer, Ramón, 61, 72

Seville, 23, 25, 33

Sitges, 95

socialists, *see* PSOE

socialist youth movement, *see* Juventudes Socialistas

Solchaga, General, 66

Soria, 31, 39

Soviet Union, 46, 57, 58, 86, 94

Spanish empire, 6, 7–8, 9

Spanish Republic, first, 12; second, 17, 83, 90, 99, 111; and agrarian reform, 16; and the Catholic Church, 15; creation of, 10–11; internal conflicts, 36, 37, 48, 60, 75, 81, 84, 87, 100, 102, 113, 114; and the Left, 17, 26, 33; reaction to the rising, 39–40, 42; and the Right, 17, 25

Talavera de la Reina, 49

Tarragona, 95

Technical Committee, 55, 80, 85

Teruel, 32, 45, 83–4

Tetuán, 28

Texas Oil Company, 82

Toledo, the *alcazar*, 49–51

Tortosa, 89

Tremp, 90–1

UGT, 17, 21, 77

Uniò Democrática, 74

Unión General de Trabajadores, *see* UGT

Unión Militar Española, 23

Uruguay, 58

USA, 113

Valencia, 26, 34, 45, 59, 89, 104,

108

Valladolid, 31, 32, 39
Varela, General Enrique, 33, 50
Vatican, 82
Vinaroz, 87
Vitoria, 31
Vizcaya, 32, 45, 65–9, 80; *see also* Basque Country

Warlimont, Lieutenant General Walter, 48

Yagüe Blanco, Lieutenant Colonel Juan, 29, 43, 50, 90, 96

Zaragoza, 25, 32, 35, 82